SCHOOL OF ORIEN

Unive

This book is due for return not _____ ___ ___ last date stamped below.
A fine will be charged for late return.

_____ enewal should be made on or before the due date,
_____ ost or by e-mail to
_____ or by telephone to 0171-323 6009.
_____ de number.

About the author

Saskia Everts is a sociologist specializing in gender studies. Now the senior consultant on gender at TOOLConsult, she lectured in gender and technology at Twente University for twelve years. She has done project management, training and policy formation on gender and technology in Burkina Faso, India, Indonesia, Ghana, Kenya and Zimbabwe

GENDER AND TECHNOLOGY
Empowering Women, Engendering Development

Saskia Everts

TOOLConsult
AMSTERDAM

Zed Books Ltd
LONDON & NEW YORK

Gender and Technology: Empowering women, engendering development was first published by Zed Books Ltd, 7 Cynthia Street, London N1 9JF, UK and Room 400, 175 Fifth Avenue, New York, NY 10010, USA in 1998.

Distributed in the USA exclusively by St Martin's Press, Inc., 175 Fifth Avenue, New York, NY 10010, USA.

Cover designed by Andrew Corbett
Set in Baskerville and Univers by Ewan Smith
Printed and bound in the United Kingdom
by Biddles Ltd, Guildford and King's Lynn

A catalogue record for this book is available from the British Library

Library of Congress Cataloging-in-Publication Data

Everts, Saskia Irene.
    Gender and technology : empowering women, engendering development / Saskia Everts.
        p.   cm.
    Includes bibliographical references (p.) and index.
    ISBN 1-85649-657-0. — ISBN 1-85649-658-9 (pbk.)
    1. Women in development. 2. Technology transfer. 3. Women-owned business enterprises—Technological innovations.   I. Title
HQ1240.E93   1998
306.4'6'082—dc21   98-29912
                                                            CIP

ISBN 1 85649 657 0 cased
ISBN 1 85649 658 9 limp

Contents

Preface

In the field of development, the theme of gender and technology receives little attention, in spite of the great importance of technological change in development, the enormous, often negative, influence of technological change on women, and the potential positive role it could play for women.

This book brings together a number of analyses and descriptions of intervention strategies in gender and technology in an attempt to contribute to a greater and more effective awareness of gender aspects of technological development. Many of the experiences described were gained during the project on Gender, Technology and Economic Empowerment, implemented from 1994 to 1997 by the development organizations TOOL and TOOLConsult in Amsterdam, and funded by NEDA, Netherlands Development Assistance (Department of International Affairs). This book shares the results of the main activities of this project.

Chapter 1 discusses the ways in which technology (defined as 'the human-made artefacts/processes and their social contexts that are geared towards enhancing human capabilities') can have an impact on women's gender needs. It presents a systematization of the issues involved, and characterizes possible strategies for improving women's situation. The focus is on women as *users* of technologies.

Women may be users of technologies in their productive, reproductive and community management roles. As to women's productive role, it is useful to distinguish between labourers, entrepreneurs and unpaid family workers. For each of these roles and work situations the (possible) impacts of technology are examined. It is shown that technology usually has two 'faces': it can appear as a potential ally, and as a potential threat to women. Each of these requires certain strategies for providing for women's gender needs.

With regard to women as *entrepreneurs*, for example, one strategy makes use of technology as an ally by strengthening women's enterprises through the introduction of improved technologies. However, for women entrepreneurs technology can be also a potential threat, because if their access to improved technologies is limited, the technology that others have can become a source of competition to women. This can happen, for example, when development projects that promote technical development of the small enterprise sector are not sufficiently gender-sensitive, so that they target only men, or have unintended adverse impacts on the situation of women. A relevant strategy here would be to promote gender awareness among development staff providing enterprise support.

Chapter 2 focuses on the introduction of 'improved' technologies into women's enterprises. From a short review of activities and information, it concludes that the main bottleneck is not so much the development or adaptation of machines, but rather the dissemination of improved technologies to more than a few women. The success of such technology dissemination is determined by the appropriateness (such as business economic appropriateness) and the accessibility of a technology. Establishing appropriateness requires forms of feasibility research, linkages between suppliers and intended users (including market-based linkages), and an iterative process. Three of the barriers to achieving appropriateness are: traditional performance indicators, characteristics of technology institutes, and gender issues in these institutions.

The accessibility of a technology requires adequate information, financing, training, organization, as well as the availability of hardware. Finally, the time dimension should be taken into account: all requirements for successful technology dissemination should also be in place in the future, in order to achieve a sustainable technology improvement.

While written material on experiences with and guidelines for successful technology dissemination could be improved, the greater need is to ensure that such texts have an influence on the practice of development work, for example through training programmes and certain institutional measures.

The next two chapters address in more detail possible means of intervening in order to increase women's empowerment through improved technologies. Chapter 3 describes a training for inter-mediate organizations that support women's small enterprises with the introduction of new technologies. The training is based on a list of the factors that need to be considered in judging whether a technology would be useful. Main topics of the training include the business aspects of introducing technology, and the gender gap in technology. Try-outs in Ghana have shown that the training can be effective in addressing a number of gaps in the knowledge of project officers and development workers involved in technology transfer to women.

Chapter 4 explores ways to catalyse market-driven dynamics of technology development, and explores possibilities of making women central actors in such dynamics. In the development and dis-semination of improved tools for women, market forces can be a most useful ally, complementary to more conventional strategies for technology development. Through market forces, some of the work of development organizations can be taken on by decentralized mechanisms that enrol the capacities of hundreds of individual entrepreneurs and customers. The ILO/TOOL programme 'FIT', which promotes farming and food-processing technologies, is testing out such approaches.

However, the market forces approach is most probably not gender-neutral. In other words: it is certainly not obvious that women can benefit as much from this approach as men can. Therefore, it should be considered from the beginning how such an approach will work out for women. The chapter discusses two examples: 'user-led innova-tion meetings', and making use of the resources of larger companies.

User-led innovation meetings bring together *users* of tools (such as farmers or food processors) and *suppliers* of tools (such as informal sector metal workers), so that the users can persuade the producers to address their specific needs. There are at least two important gender issues here. One is the issue of women's *access* to user-led innovation meetings. The design of a user-led innovation meeting should take into account all the general provisions that are necessary to enable women to participate in any meeting, such as choice of time, place and occasion of the meeting. The second issue is women's 'consumer power'. It is necessary to know the extent of women's control over and access to income within the household. Thus, a basic knowledge of *intra-household dynamics* is indispensable when trying to promote user-led innovation in agricultural tools in a gender-sensitive way. Next to income level and control over finances, *information* and *attitudes* determine the degree of women's consumer power.

Another way of using market forces as an ally is to try to make use of the resources of larger companies. These resources can be large, and many companies also have an impressive infrastructure that already reaches down to many people. Larger companies have their own reasons for being interested in co-operation with development organizations, such as their corporate image, or the fact that helping customers may eventually increase their market. The challenge in 'tapping the industry channel' is to find where the interests of development organizations and large companies overlap. It is important, however, carefully to avoid negative side-effects, for example contributing to the competition that some companies pose to micro- and small-scale enterprises (MSEs) that one wants to support. There are many forms of co-operation that actually have the potential to strengthen the small entrepreneurs or farmers reached, but it should never be taken for granted that an effective plan will be as effective for women as it is for men. A gender analysis of the target group can give an explanation of why an intervention may reach significantly fewer women. It will also give ideas on how a programme could be readjusted to increase the chances of benefiting women. Five steps are described with which it is possible to start to 'tap the industry channel' in order to help a specific target group, such as women food processors.

The second part of the book focuses on mainstreaming gender concerns into technological development through training, gender analysis and gender sensitization. It presents a number of examples and strategies of mainstreaming activities.

A 'gender integration trajectory', which was tried out during the TOOL/TOOLConsult project, is described in Chapter 5. The trajectory is based on a situation, present in many development organizations, in which there is a basically positive attitude towards gender integration which is hindered by a number of barriers. The gender-integration trajectory addresses these barriers. The trajectory includes both training and the development and implementation of a short, time-efficient gender analysis instrument (the Efficient Gender Analysis or EGA). The EGA is an instrument with which projects can be systematically analysed in a short time, and recommendations for improvement can be generated. It consists of questions on the objectives, the activities and the results of projects, and can also be used for technical projects that do not seem to involve people at all. The training mainly focuses on increasing *skills* of gender integration. Gender *awareness* and *knowledge* of gender issues are dealt with when these themes arise naturally from the gender-integration activities. All in all, the gender-integration trajectory has developed a number of pragmatic alternatives to traditional approaches in mainstreaming.

Chapters 6 and 7 describe a number of project activities directed at gender-sensitizing engineers in the South. Marie C. Fry has designed and given gender training to large groups of engineers from the Ministry of Agriculture in Bangladesh, as well as to irrigation and hydraulics engineers from Vietnam. Realistically limited targets, working with the management and trying to speak the language of engineers proved to be crucial factors in their success. Chapter 7 by Josef Kienzle, Megan Lloyd-Laney and Saskia Everts recounts the programme of AGSE, the Agricultural Engineering Section of the FAO, which has combined a workshop, a series of interviews and a booklet of case studies to gender-sensitize those agricultural engineers who (although they may feel guilty about it) are not convinced of the importance of gender.

Part Two closes with two analyses of specific technical domains in which gender issues have only very recently been addressed. Priyanthi Fernando addresses rural transport and identifies the unequal distribution of the transport burden, the unequal access to transport technologies and the invisibility of women's transport needs in transport planning as three key issues relating to gender and rural transport. Integration of gender into rural transport interventions requires the participation of women in both the planning process and in the design of the interventions. Moreover, strategies for women's empowerment should also address access and mobility issues. What is needed is a better identification of problems, more interventions, greater understanding of impacts and increased women's participation.

Maria S. Muller's analysis addresses gender issues in urban waste management. These gender issues are visible on three levels: there are gender aspects related to waste as a source of income, gender aspects related to waste as a health and environment hazard, and gender aspects of defining community needs and promoting community participation. The needs of women and men from one community regarding waste management are likely to differ from each other, given their different lives and responsibilities. In fact, what is seen as waste and what as a resource is often different for men and women; in other words, the definition of waste itself is gendered. Waste management projects should address the factors that limit women's opportunities, together with specific waste management requirements. In this way NGOs and other development organizations can break through the vicious circle in which disadvantaged groups benefit less from development than the already advantaged groups.

Historically, the process of development, particularly of technological development, has been strongly influenced by men. This gender bias has affected the role of women in the development process, and in many cases has led to the introduction of technologies that are beneficial and suited to men, but much less so to women. Sometimes technological development has had a clear detrimental effect on the position of women.

In the past, it was a generally accepted idea that technological developments would automatically lead to increased and equally distributed welfare and well-being at all levels. The opposite has been the case: sometimes women's positions have worsened as a consequence of mechanization processes which made them lose control of profitable income-generating activities.

Technology is nevertheless an important motor for development, and can in principle be a substantial force in improving women's lives in many respects, such as reducing the amount of heavy work to be carried out, increasing access to information and mobility, and increasing opportunities for income generation. A few projects have indeed provided women with improved equipment. An example of such a project is the Bielenberg Oil Press in Tanzania, which became one of the better-known success stories in the history of transfer of appropriate technology.

Although within development work more attention is paid to gender issues than in many other policy fields, very little has changed so far regarding gender, development and technology. Technology has been an underdeveloped theme within gender and development, and engineers are among the last development workers to realize that gender issues are also relevant to their work. Since technological changes form a substantial part of most development initiatives, it is high time to increase drastically the efforts to get a grip on the gender effects of technological development.

Funded by the Dutch development department NEDA, a project was started in 1994 to contribute to the further pursuit of gender issues in technology development. The project was taken on by TOOL, originally an AT organization and now an information broker on technology and development, and implemented by its sister organization TOOLConsult, which specializes in gender and technology, as well as in non-financial services for small-scale enterprises, and in energy and environment issues. Saskia Everts was hired to carry out the project.

In this two-year project, approaches were developed for the integration of gender into technology-related projects, such as the projects in which TOOL and TOOLConsult themselves are involved. The project activities included: an analysis of the theme 'gender, technology and development'; an initiative to increase the attention for gender in the own organization (TOOL and TOOLConsult); the development of training on the ins and outs of technology transfer to women's enterprises (which was tried out in Ghana); and a conference where not only these activities were presented, but also the experiences of a group of other gender and technology experts. This book is based on all these activities and is intended to share the main findings and results with a wider audience.

Gender activities in development can be divided into two forms. The first kind are the activities that specifically target women in an effort to strengthen their position. These are 'women's projects' or sometimes 'women's components' added on to general projects. An activity that supports projects which specifically target women is described in Chapter 3.

Most development projects and programmes, however, do not specifically target women. Rather, the beneficiaries are 'farmers' or 'entrepreneurs', or the objective is 'to improve the environment' or 'to increase access to clean water'. It may be the (implicit) intention that women are among the beneficiaries, but it is not the specific aim of such projects to reach women *in particular*. The second kind of gender activities is directed at these general projects and is called mainstreaming. The aim is to take gender issues into account in such projects, to make the project more effective and to ensure that women also benefit from it.

Because so much of the development work and money is chan-
nelled into such general projects, their effects on women are of great
importance. Gender issues must be mainstreamed into such general
projects to ensure that women benefit from them. Technology-related
development work in particular is mostly 'general'. Thus, if women
are to benefit more from technological development, mainstreaming
is one of the important tasks to be undertaken.

Mainstreaming requires approaching the non-gender experts who
are involved in development work, such as the (usually male) engineers in both the North and the South, with, for example, training,
information, instruments and advice. Part Two of this book recounts
a number of cases that demonstrate ways to tackle this task of
'engendering development'.

This book is written for everyone involved in technological development and in gender and development. Practitioners, whether at
the policy level (such as donors) or at the intermediate level (such as
NGOs), as well as academics with a practical interests, are invited to
take whatever they find of use from the analyses and experiences in
this book and integrate it in their own work.

Acknowledgements

The writing of this book, as well as many of the activities described in it, were made possible by a financial contribution from the Netherlands Development Assistance (NEDA, formerly called DGIS) through the project 'Gender, Technology and Economic Empowerment'. Responsibility for the contents and for the opinions expressed rests solely with the author. Publication does not constitute an endorsement by NEDA.

Four of the chapters have been written by or in co-operation with other authors. Each of these chapters is based on a paper written for the TOOL/TOOLConsult conference, 'Technology and Development, Strategies for the Integration of Gender', held in Amsterdam on 5–6 June 1997, and organized by the author as part of the above-named project. I wish to thank Ita Muller of WASTE, Pryanthi Fernando of the International Forum for Rural Transport and Development (IFRTD), Marie Fry, private consultant, Josef Kienzle of FAO and Megan Lloyd-Laney, private consultant, for giving me permission to edit or rewrite their papers for inclusion in this book.

Earlier versions of some of the chapters have been published elsewhere. Shortened versions of Chapters 2 and 8 appeared in Vol. 2, No. 1 of *Gender, Technology and Development*, January–May 1998, published by Sage India. Earlier versions of Chapter 9 were presented at the programme policy meeting at the Urban Waste Expertise Programme, organized by WASTE in Gouda, the Netherlands, in 1997; contributions to this chapter from Usha P. Raghupathi, Associate Professor at the National Institute of Urban Affairs, New Delhi, are gratefully acknowledged. Chapter 4 was first written, with the financial support of the FAO and the ILO/TOOLConsult FIT Programme, for the FAO/AGROTEC workshop, 'Gender and Agricultural Engineering', held in Kadoma, Zimbabwe, in March 1996.

I wish to thank my colleagues, both in and outside TOOL and TOOLConsult, for their support, as well as for their occasional resistance to the gender-message, without either of which this book would certainly have been less informed.

Finally, I dedicate the book to my son Jowán van Lente, who has made me discover some baffling but wonderful aspects – which I had not known before – of being a woman.

Abbreviations

AGSE   Agricultural Engineering Section of the FAO
AT   Appropriate Technology
ATI   Appropriate Technology International (a Washington
              DC-based NGO)
DAE   Department of Agricultural Extension (Bangladesh)
EAI   East African Industries
EGA   Efficient Gender Analysis
FAO   Food and Agricultural Organization
FARMESA   Farm-level Applied Research Methods for East and
              Southern Africa (a SIDA-funded FAO field programme)
FIT   Farm Implements and Tools (an ILO/TOOLConsult
              development programme)
GAD   gender and development
GREP   Gender Responsive Extension Programming
IFAD   International Fund for Agricultural Development
IFRTD   International Forum for Rural Transport and
              Development
ILO   International Labour Organization
IRAP   Integrated Rural Accessibility Planning
IRC   International Water and Sanitation Centre
IRTP   Integrated Rural Transport Planning
ITDG   Intermediate Technology Development Group
MSE   micro- and small-scale enterprise
NCWD   National Council on Women and Development (from
              the government of Ghana)
NEDA   Netherlands Development Assistance (formerly called
              DGIS)
NGO   non-governmental organization
PRA   Participatory Rural Appraisal

PROWESS	Promotion of the Role of Women in Water and Environmental Sanitation Services
SNV	Netherlands Development Organization
RMA	Rapid Market Appraisal
SADC	Southern African Development Community
SEWA	Self-Employed Women's Association
SIDA	Swedish International Development Agency
SSE	small-scale enterprise
TOOL	Technology for Development (an NGO)
TOOLConsult	the independently operating consultancy department of the NGO TOOL
ToR	terms of reference
TOT	training of trainers
UNIDO	United Nations Industrial Development Organization
UNIFEM	United Nations Development Fund for Women
UNDP	United Nations Development Programme
UWEP	Urban Waste Expertise Programme
WAFT	Women and Food Technologies (a UNIFEM programme)
WASTE	advisors on Urban Environment and Development (a Dutch NGO)
WID	women in development

Part One
Empowering Women

1. Technology and gender needs: an overview

This chapter introduces the issue of technology and gender needs, particularly in relation to women's economic empowerment. Gender and technology comprise a broad range of themes. Focusing mainly on women as *users* of technology, this chapter orders the broad range of questions, issues and problems that can be seen as belonging to this terrain, and identifies possibilities for interventions. The first section discusses the terms 'gender needs' and 'technology', and presents some typologies that can be used to order the field. 'Issues and strategies' provides an overview of various ways in which technology impinges on women's lives, and delineates some basic strategies for monitoring the influence of technology on gender needs.

Definitions and typologies

Gender needs   Gender needs are 'needs that women (or men for that matter) may develop by virtue of their social positioning through gender attributes' (Molyneux 1985, cited in Moser 1993: 38). In this definition, both men and women have gender needs. This chapter focuses on the gender needs of women. Why has the term 'women's *gender* needs' been chosen rather than just 'women's needs'? The needs discussed here (for economic empowerment, for securing higher incomes, for reduction of drudgery, for improved health and suitable employment) could just as well be presented as women's needs. However, to talk about (women's) 'gender needs' rather than just 'women's needs' emphasizes how women and their needs are viewed; it reminds us that these needs arise out of the social positioning of

3

women in the gender structure: a culturally constructed inequality between men and women. The need for more egalitarian gender relations underlies many of women's gender needs.

The term 'gender' also acknowledges that the specific contents and meanings of male/female differentiation are culturally and historically determined, and that they can change. The fulfilment of gender needs in fact often contributes to changes in the gender structure. To illustrate this, Moser distinguishes between *practical* gender needs, 'the needs identified to help women in their existing subordinate position', and *strategic* gender needs, 'the needs identified to transform existing subordinate relationships between men and women' (Moser 1993: 94). The latter aim should be the ultimate objective.

In this discussion of technology and gender needs, special attention has been paid to *economic* empowerment. Economic empowerment has been widely identified as a strategic factor in improving women's position. Moreover, women in developing countries consistently identify economic needs as one of their main priorities (see, for example, Carr 1984: 5). The main issue in this book is how technology interacts with such gender needs: how technology does, or could, contribute to or hamper their fulfilment, how it might create new gender needs, and the ways in which gender needs can be taken into account when dealing with technology.

Technology Technology plays a central role in the development process. In fact, technology and progress are often regarded as more or less synonymous. However, it has been widely argued that technological inputs in developing countries (and also in more developed countries) have not benefited women much, or at least not as much as men, and have often actually harmed them (Mies and Shiva 1993). At the same time, others have stressed the need to transfer technologies as a means of improving women's lives (Jain 1985). Thus, whether or not specific technologies bring progress – and to whom and for which aspects of their lives – can vary substantially. Regarding gender and technology, it is important to analyse how technological changes (could) benefit women and why they sometimes harm them.

What is meant in fact by technology? There is no consensus on how technology should be defined. The definition we adopt is not unimportant, since in the choice of a particular definition certain issues are included in discussions and in actions, and others are excluded and therefore ignored. Here, technology is considered as a potential aid, as this book is concerned with the ways in which technology can help to fulfil needs. Thus, the *instrumental* character of technology is essential; it should be clear that we talk about objects and processes that (can) help humans, that mediate in human action, or 'that enhance human capabilities' (Stamp 1989). Interestingly, placing 'enhancement' in the definition of technology is at the same time problematic because in certain specific cases technology may not 'enhance' any capabilities. For example, does the technology of the automobile in the context of the city of Bangkok enhance human capabilities? And if it does (maybe if not through enabling rapid transport then, for example, by enabling privacy), does it enhance more capabilities than it reduces on some other dimension (for example, the reduction of the possibility of social contacts en route, or for spontaneous or emergency visits)? For whom does it enhance capabilities, and whose capabilities may be reduced in the process? This is exactly the point that needs to be debated, since technology and progress are not synonymous. Nevertheless, technology will here be defined by its ideal characteristic of being geared towards enhancing capabilities, while in practice the question will each time be posed whether some concrete technology actually does this.

When we define technology as an object that 'does something', that 'works' or 'helps', it is defined through *the way it functions*. But no tool or artefact functions just by itself. Imagine a television, for example, taken from a town in Mongolia on the back of a horse into the Mongolian steppes, such as happened in the movie *Urga*. Since a technology always 'does something', a television apparatus is only a technology if it does something. It only does the things that we think of a television as doing if all kinds of other conditions are in place (energy supply, broadcasting company, someone who knows how to turn it on, someone who wants to turn it on, etc.). If these conditions are not in place, the television will not do anything and it is no longer a technology, or not one of the kind that the makers intended (it may, for example, be used as a table, and in that sense be a tool).

An object in itself, however well designed with the purpose of enhancing human capabilities, cannot be called a technology but is merely an artefact, an object or a thing. What *is* to be called 'technology' is the total package of this artefact plus the organizational, informational and human contexts that are required for its functioning. Taking this into account, technology will be defined as *the human-made artefacts/processes and their social contexts that are geared towards enhancing human capabilities.*

Through this definition, the social context of technology is included in every discussion or action about technology. For example, it becomes automatically clear that 'technology transfer' is not simply 'bringing a machine to another place'. Technology transfer is bringing the machine plus bringing or creating the necessary organization, information and human context, without which the machine does nothing.

This definition also forces us to think differently about the *effects* of technology. It becomes evident that any impact that seems to arise from a technology (or even directly from an artefact), in fact arises from the interplay between a technology and the social context that surrounds it. As to the outcome of the interaction between technology and the wider context, no general predictions can be made. It is clear that sometimes technology has the potential to bring about enormous changes in social relations, yet the technology can also be 'modified' by the wider context. A tool can be used in a variety of ways, and may wind up changing very little. For example, research has shown that the time women in Western countries spend on household chores and child care has changed remarkably little during the twentieth century, despite the invention and dissemination of labour-saving household devices. One reason for this is that, while the time required to perform a particular task may have diminished, somehow the demand for better quality has increased just as much (Cowan 1983). Thus the effects of an artefact can vary widely depending on the context in which it functions.

The term 'technology' will be used as an umbrella term to include all kinds of technologies. A technology can be 'high-' or 'low-tech', complex or simple. It may have been used for a long time or be newly developed. Extensive training may be required to use it, or it may be understood easily. For most people, however, the term 'technology' is associated with 'difficult', 'complex' and 'new'. These associations cause us to think of some technologies as being 'more' technological, or more 'real technologies', than others, and cause us to ignore some artefacts that may enhance human capabilities just as much. Shoes, for example, can in some circumstances be very important tools for women to help them do their work; and a window is an ingenious technology that manages to keep out the cold while letting in light. Both shoes and windows are artefacts that enable people to do things that would not have been possible in the same way without the artefact, and thus can be included in a discussion of technology and gender needs.

Interestingly, often exactly those things which are often used by *women* are not seen as (real) technologies. Why is someone who is good at knitting and sewing not seen as technical? How technical do we see devices for carrying babies? Certainly, the term 'technology' is often associated with 'masculine'. Such associations are often value-laden. In the context of this book, where one of the issues is how technologies could contribute to the alleviation of gender needs, it is wise to try to include *any* technology that is geared to the enhancement of human capabilities.

Women as users and producers of technologies It is useful to distinguish between women as users and as producers of technology. Both of these can be discussed under the heading 'gender and technology', and they are related. However, the concerns, situations and possible strategic interventions are very different. This book mainly deals with the different ways in which women are or could be *users* of technologies, and how this affects gender needs. When speaking of users or consumers of technology, we should not only think of women (and men) in the home, in the private or non-productive sphere, using for example radios, bicycles or cooking utensils. Men and women are also users of technologies when they are active in *production* processes (e.g. in small businesses producing clothes or food). A tailor or food producer is on the one hand a 'producer' (of clothes or of jam), and on the other hand a *user* (one could even say consumer) of the sewing machine or the food processor used in the production process.

The issue of women as *users* of technology also includes women whom we could call 'non-users'. In other words, the question why some groups of women do *not* use some technologies is equally relevant; this raises for instance the issue of accessibility of technologies.

Women (like men, but more so) more frequently come into contact with technology as users than as producers. However, women can also be *producers of technology*, such as those who construct wood-saving ovens, run an iron forge, or are involved in the design of a communal latrine (where the oven and the latrine are regarded as technologies and we assume that the forge makes tools). To complicate matters, such technology producers are often also users of other technologies involved in such tool production. In other words, in one activity women can use one technology and at the same time produce another. For example, women working in factories producing computer chips are technology producers in the sense that they are involved in producing computer technology, but are also technology *users* in that they work with an industrial production process – comparable to, for example, women in the confectionery industry. In this particular case, women's user-status will probably be more relevant in defining their relation to the technology than their producer role. But we could in principle focus on each of these roles.

The issue of women as *producers* of technology includes a number of important questions:

- What kind of (indigenous) technologies have women developed?
- Why are women under-represented among producers of technology?
- To what extent does this under-representation influence the kinds of technologies that are produced?
- How could women benefit from a greater involvement in technology production?
- How can more women be drawn into technology production (e.g. into technical education), or increase their participation in technology design (e.g. through participatory technology development or through forms of consumer testing)?
- How can women gain greater access to the channels through which the development of technology can be influenced?

Regarding women as users, a first question is in which ways women's lives touch upon different technologies.

The three roles of women   Women may be users of technology in all areas of their lives. For women in the Third World, Moser identifies three roles: productive, reproductive and community management: '*The productive role* comprises work done [...] for payment in cash or in kind. It includes both market production with an exchange value, and subsistence/home production with an actual use-value, but also a potential exchange value' (Moser 1993: 24). In spite of the word 'productive', the productive role must be seen as including both production (industry, agriculture) and services (office work, trade, teaching, government service, running a restaurant). Women carry out their productive role in various work situations. Grijns et al. (1992) give a useful schematic representation of these work situations, distinguishing between the entrepreneur, the labourer and the unpaid family worker. The entrepreneur includes a wide range of forms of self-employment: from the large-scale owner and employer in the modern sector, to the irregular household production of some surplus goods for trade or barter. Grijns et al. note that these three employment situations, rather than being clearly dif-ferentiated forms of production, form a kind of circle:

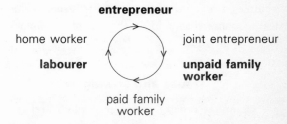

Between each of these categories there are borderline cases, such as paid family workers, and women who form joint enterprises with their husbands. Between the categories of entrepreneur and labourer there is the group of women in certain forms of subcontracting relations, notably home workers (sometimes called domestic out-workers [Grijns et al. 1992: 195]). Technology inputs in their productive role could help women to set up or improve a business (for women entrepreneurs) or to make their work less arduous.

'*The reproductive role* comprises the childbearing/rearing responsi-bilities and domestic tasks undertaken by women, required to guarantee the maintenance and reproduction of the labour force' (Moser 1993: 26). The difference between the productive and the reproductive activities is *not* that the first kind of activity *produces* something while the second does not, for production takes place also in the reproductive role (for example the production of food). Nor is the difference that the reproductive role has no use-value. What distinguishes reproductive work from other work is the context in which it is done: the direct beneficiaries are members of the household, and in that sense the work has no economic exchange value. Relevant to this role are drudgery-reducing technologies for women's work.

'*The community management role* comprises activities undertaken primarily by women at the community level, as an extension of their reproductive role. This is to ensure the provision and maintenance of scarce resources of collective consumption, such as water, health care and education. It is voluntary unpaid work' (Moser 1993: 28–36). In this role, women are touched by technologies such as water supply, medical technologies and technologies that impinge on the environment. Men also have a role in the community, but this role centres around the formal and public political level and is more often renumerated (in money or in kind).

These three roles of women are used to structure the discussion in the next sections, which address the role of technology in each of the main forms of women's activities.

Issues and strategies

To get a grasp on the broad issue of 'technology and gender needs', it is necessary to present a systematization of the many different issues that it includes. This section does so by noting that technology impinges on the gender needs of women in each of their main roles. Within each of these roles, technology can be regarded both as an opportunity and as a potential threat. Both to avoid technology's potential threats and optimally to use its potential opportunity to meet the needs of women, a number of strategies are available.

Women entrepreneurs Most women's enterprises are micro- or small-scale, providing work for the women themselves and possibly some family members. Working capital is limited and profit margins are low (see Grijns et al. 1992: viii; Baud et al. 1993: 9, 109–11). Such businesses are flexible, and the work may be part-time and/or seasonal, as shown by the following example described by Grijns et al. (1992):

Ibu Enis works with bamboo most of the week, but at irregular intervals, usually a few hours in the early morning. She then stops to attend to the household tasks of cooking, washing and the like, but resumes work in the afternoon. The work of Ibu Enis is frequently interrupted by the demands of the children, especially of the youngest who is still a baby. The work intensifies when urgent orders need to be delivered at short notice. (Grijns et al. 1992: 145)

Women's businesses are often located in, or run from, the home and provide essential sources of income for the household. Such enterprises are security- rather than growth-oriented (Downing 1991). Some women also operate small- , medium- and even large-scale enterprises. These women have specific needs that arise from their position as women (Parikh 1991).

Women entrepreneurs and technology Technology is relevant to many women's enterprises, particularly those in sectors such as food and drinks processing, manufacturing (e.g. soap making, utensil making), or in agriculture. But technology is also relevant in the trade sector, in which many women have enterprises. For example, access to transport, or even to weighing-scales, can determine women's business success to an extent (Everts 1982).

As is the case for all micro- or informal sector enterprises in developing countries, women's micro-enterprises have high labour and low capital inputs, which imply a low technology input. In some sectors, women's enterprises are poorly equipped technologically compared with those run by men making similar products. Such a split production sector can arise when new technologies become available, but find their way more easily into men's businesses. For some women's businesses this may lead to the loss of customers, although sometimes they retain a section of the market by supplying, for example, cheaper or lower-quality products.

Technology as an opportunity Technology can be seen as an op-portunity to improve women's businesses, leading to increases in production, to new or changed products, or to products of higher quality. Such improvements could lead to higher profits, and to greater security and/or autonomy for women. This view of techno-logy as an opportunity for fulfilling gender needs has been adopted by many (development) project initiatives. Strategies to use this oppor-tunity involve innovation, technology transfer and dissemination, or 'the harnessing of technology for women's needs' (Jain 1985). The next chapter discusses such strategies in detail. Here it will also be shown that higher quality or quantity production is not automatically an improvement, although the terms are sometimes used almost synonymously. Whether or not a new technology is an improvement for a woman's business is in large part the economic, market-related question of whether there can or will be returns on the technological investment.

Technology as a threat The negative influence of technology on women's enterprises is often indirect. Technologies are not only consciously brought to or adopted by women; technological change within the wider environment also affects them. At the macro-level, technology is relevant to women's enterprises in that it often represents a source of competition. For example, new production technologies introduced in rich countries can threaten the businesses of women in developing countries; indeed, entire sectors can lose their markets to new, better or cheaper goods.

At the micro-level, the threat to women's enterprises can arise when efficiency-improving technology is less accessible to women than to men working in comparable sectors. One of the sources of this gender-based differential access to improved technologies can be traced to gender bias in development assistance. In many programmes involving technology transfer or providing enterprise support, technologies have often been introduced in such a way that they have benefited male entrepreneurs at the expense of competing women's businesses, as the following example cited by Ahmed (1985) demonstrates:

> [In the past] all along coastal India women could be seen marketing head loads of fresh fish. Preservation techniques like salting and drying, which increased the shelf-life of fish, were also mainly in the hands of rural women. However, the Integrated Fisheries Development Programme in Kerala India, uses trawlers to catch prawns, which are frozen and exported. Factories have been built to process and freeze the prawns and fish, and men have taken over the marketing and transportation of fish using trucks and bicycles. Rural women's jobs and livelihoods from fish trading and processing have been lost, and there are no alternative sources of income or employment. (Ahmed 1985: 323)

Strategies One possible strategy to counter the differential access of male and female entrepreneurs to technical options could be to address the main factors that determine access to technology: information and the availability of credit. Development initiatives aiming to improve technology transfer could, for example, provide credit programmes for women, gender training for bank personnel, or technology source books. Chapter 2 gives a more detailed discussion of the issue of access.

In the case where the threat of competition is generated by development initiatives themselves, one answer is to increase gender awareness among development workers. This strategy, known as 'mainstreaming', involves integrating an awareness of gender relations, and of the needs of women arising from those gender relations, into the 'mainstream' of development work. This means that programme designers become more aware of the consequences to women of *all* initiatives that involve technological change, even if women are not specifically targeted. The general idea of mainstreaming gender in technology-related development initiatives is further discussed in Chapter 5.

Efforts to 'mainstream' gender have been increasing since the late 1980s. 'Mainstream' initiatives do not explicitly aim at meeting gender needs. For example, rather than intending to improve the situation of women entrepreneurs, a mainstream project would be aiming to support small enterprises in general. In such enterprise-support projects, technology is almost always relevant, for example, where the support includes improving the capacity for innovation, technology assessments and decision-making on purchases of technology, and where design and transfer of appropriate production technologies are included. Other mainstream projects that are relevant from the point of view of gender and technology include those that support the tool-making sector.

Such projects need to integrate knowledge and awareness of how interventions can affect women's businesses. In fact, by ignoring gender needs, projects may be harmful to women (or at least to their position relative to that of men). In a useful text on this subject, *Guidebook for Integrating Women into Small and Micro Enterprise Projects*, Otero (1987) discusses the specific need to support women's businesses. She lists a number of ways in which women could be included in project assistance, and addresses the point of '*de facto* selectivity': the implicit selection of men's enterprises as the beneficiaries of support. Her guidelines for preventing such selectivity are worth quoting here:

> When there is a low proportion of women in the pool of eligibles for project assistance, women's participation tends to be low, in spite of active efforts to include them. Three steps can be taken to prevent this type of *de facto* selectivity from occurring: (1) Expand the eligibility criteria. (2) Consider developing a special women's component designed to respond to the constraints that render women ineligible. (3) Institute an active recruitment programme for women (particularly effective when implicit exclusion, based on cultural perceptions, reduces the number of eligible women; explicit exclusion is the contrary state). (Otero 1987)

If a greater effort can be made to include women in general enterprise support projects, women can benefit from such initiatives, rather than be threatened by them.

In summary, the opportunities offered by technology to meet the gender needs of entrepreneurs call for the development of strategies to utilize them to the full. The threats to women's enterprises posed by technological change, especially change arising from development initiatives, need to be monitored carefully. They could (at least in principle) be circumvented or turned to advantage through counter-strategies to ensure that women's gender needs are taken fully into account in the design and implementation of projects for all small-scale entrepreneurs.

Women labourers Women labourers include those who are employed full-time to day-labourers. Industrial wage labour, like traditional work, is highly sex-segregated and also age-segregated. Everywhere, women are found in disproportionately high numbers in the lowest paid and least secure jobs. Especially in small- and medium-scale enterprises, women's work is frequently heavy and health threatening.

Between the 'labourer' and the 'entrepreneur' lies the homeworker. She may work at home and at her own pace, yet she may be dependent on an enterprise that collects (or buys) the product, provides (or sells) the raw materials, and sometimes owns the production technology. This dependency makes it difficult to determine whether such women are self-employed or wage workers. Increasing numbers of companies are organizing their production through such sub-contracting relations.

Women labourers and technology Most labourers are users of technologies, so that any changes in those technologies are bound to have some influence on (women) workers and possibly also on gender relations. Again, technology can be seen as a potential benefit or opportunity, and as a potential threat to the gender needs of women.

Health and safety One of the most important 'promises' that technology in principle holds for women workers is that it will improve their health and safety. However, for women labourers such technological changes would have to be introduced by their employers. The question is then how employers can be encouraged to adopt such technological improvements in a sustainable way. In other words, what room for manoeuvre exists for those who wish to improve women's working conditions, and what strategies are likely to be most effective?

It seems that employers must either recognize the economic benefits of such improvements, or be coerced (by governments in the form of regulations, or by labour unions) into taking action to improve the health and safety of their employees. With regard to the economic argument, the relevant question is: under what conditions could health and safety improvements be made, while at the same time improving the efficiency of the business and thus the economic returns? Most small enterprises are unlikely to have the financial means to make provisions of this kind, and even if they were (heavily) subsidized it is debatable whether such improvements would increase or decrease the sustainable adoption of safer technologies.

The strategy of applying pressure to employers leads to the question of whether the unionization of women would be effective. Another source of pressure could come from donors, who could make their funding dependent on the employer's behaviour. However, we can ask to what extent could, and *should*, donors and development agencies make use of the beneficiary's need 'to keep the donor happy'? Such questions are also relevant for technologies that could improve the health and safety of *male* labourers. In this respect, perhaps a study is needed of how the gender division of labour is reflected in differences in the health and safety of workers.

Home-workers represent an 'in-between' group of women labourers that is difficult to reach and sometimes even to identify. Some of these women, although *de facto* labourers, have to supply their own production equipment. It is likely that they would be willing to adopt safer and healthier technologies (provided that they are inexpensive to buy and/or maintain, and that the health benefits are clearly evident), since the women themselves would benefit.

Threat of loss of employment Technological change is a constant feature of the environment of women labourers. For example, a business employing women labourers may introduce new technologies to increase productivity, improve product quality, or to expand its market. Such technological changes have few direct advantages for (women) workers, and may even have negative effects.

One of the most important effects of technological change concerns employment. Most technological changes based on Western examples aim to reduce labour costs. As Baud notes, 'when new technology is introduced in a large enterprise, women's employment within the firm can be either increased or decreased. If the work content of jobs becomes more complex, women are usually edged out. If it is simplified, women are recruited more extensively' (Baud and de Bruijne 1993: 9). In 1967, the ILO conducted a survey of a number of sectors (metal-working; textiles, clothing, leather and footwear; food and drinks; and printing and allied trades) and found that 'in every case where machinery was introduced in activities traditionally done by women, men either completely replaced women or the activity became sub-divided and men took over the tasks that used the technology and required greater skill, while women were relegated to the less skilled, menial tasks' (Anderson 1985: 61).

This pattern has been observed in many countries, but its exact workings are difficult to grasp. Certainly, it is based on a complex interaction of psychological, symbolic and social mechanisms (Oost 1994). Could this tendency be neutralized by some kind of counter-strategy? On a small scale, concerted efforts could be made to train women employees to perform any new functions that arise from technological changes. Given the rigidity of the pattern, however, the provision of training alone may be too narrow a strategy. A full programme of action to stimulate the entry of women into non-traditional jobs may be needed (so-called 'positive action programmes'), although this would require a heavy commitment from at least some of the relevant actors. Such efforts could neutralize the threat of technology or perhaps help to turn it into an opportunity.

Unpaid family workers In many countries women, men and children work together in family-run enterprises. For example, following a study of the rural non-farm sector in Java, Sjaifudian (1992) observed:

> on the basis of the form of involvement, family workers can be said to exist along a continuum, from those who take part in management of the business and those who help in production or domestic work, to those who are apprentices. It was found in a number of cases, for example in the dairy industry, that there are women family workers who in reality run or have run a business but are not formally recognized as entrepreneurs because this position has been taken over by or transferred to the husband, the point being that family workers of this kind can really be called disguised entrepreneurs. (Sjaifudian 1992: 178)

The situation of the unpaid family worker has elements of those of both the entrepreneur and the labourer, but the balance between them depends on the situation, particularly on the degree of freedom, control and remuneration of the female family worker, and on the division of income and decision-making power among family members. If a woman works for her husband who is both *de jure* and *de facto* head of the family business, then most of the issues in the discussion of women labourers are relevant, whereas if she is part of an entrepreneurial household (sometimes there are clear-cut cases of joint entrepreneurship), then her situation is comparable with that of the self-employed.

Strategies For this reason, family workers can be approached with the same strategies described for other groups, although their specific situations should be considered when relevant. For example, family workers are harder to reach than many wage workers. Strategies that aim to make use of group pressure are less likely to be effective than those aimed at women labourers who work outside the home. Family workers are more isolated, the businesses are more difficult to track down, and it is harder to check that regulations are being complied with. Also, there is the issue of who has control over any technical

improvements and over their benefits. Since the woman is not paid
for her labour (her contribution to the family enterprise may not
even be regarded as work), any financial gain that arises from the use
of better equipment will be absorbed by the enterprise or the family
as a whole. Sometimes it is the woman who has taken out a loan for
her equipment, yet her ability to pay back the loan will depend on
the financial decision-making structure within the household.

TOOL developed with an Indian NGO a foot-driven spinning
wheel for wool spinning in India, with which wool could be spun
quicker and with less strain (the 'Medleri Charkha'). About two-
thirds of the woman spinners spin for their husbands, the weavers;
they have no private earnings from spinning. Yet it was the women
who were approached for the credit programme, and they took the
loans for the wheel, which was an important factor in increasing
their sense of independence and self-worth. The project shows that
this arrangement can work: although the women have no private
earnings, the loans are being paid back on time, from the household
income (TOOL 1994: 1).

It would be worthwhile to study family workers in more detail.
Important questions include how, on what grounds and by whom
decisions are made with regard to the introduction of technical
improvements for unpaid family workers.

Women's reproductive and community management roles

Within women's *reproductive role* the central tasks are the bearing and
socializing of children, passing on knowledge and values, caring for
both husband and children, preparing meals, washing clothes and
dishes, cleaning living spaces, taking care of the health of the family,
and collecting, growing or buying the daily household needs (including, of course, food and water). Note that these activities include
forms of production (making food), as well as activities that are more
like services (carrying a child). This work is not in any essential way
different from the work described above as 'productive' work. The
actual activities may be similar (preparing a meal, grinding corn,
weeding a field, dressing a child or giving a medicine), but it is the
social organization of the activities that makes reproductive work a
distinct kind of work. Reproductive work distinguishes itself from
other work because the direct beneficiaries are members of the
household.

The beneficiaries of the tasks performed by a woman in her *community management role* are not only the members of her direct household, but community members in general. Community management tasks, like reproductive tasks, are not renumerated economically.

Technology in women's reproductive and community management roles   Technology is relevant to many of women's reproductive activities. Examples of the technologies involved in these tasks include:

- food processing: stoves, pots, cooking utensils, means of carrying and transport, tools for conservation, for measuring, for grinding, grating, sieving, cutting, etc.;
- cleaning: means for scrubbing or washing textiles, cleaning aids;
- fetching water: water supply, means of transport, containers, sanitation;
- caring for children: carrying devices, means of improving children's health and safety.

In the context of cleaning, soap may be regarded as a tool or technology that could be improved in order to enhance human capabilities with regard to cleaning tasks. The layout of the house can also be seen as a technological way of improving or facilitating the cleaning process. (An extreme example is the 'self-cleaning house', designed and built by Frances Gabe [Zimmerman 1983].) The double doors found in many old Dutch farmhouses have been described as a technology that increases child safety. The top part of the door could be left open to let in light, fresh air and allow the woman to talk to passers-by, while the bottom half could be kept closed to prevent children wandering outside and animals strolling in. Given the way such a human-made object does something to help humans, 'to perform a task', as it were, it is a technology (using the definition given earlier); more important, however, it makes sense to explore how the object might be used or improved to help meet women's gender needs.

Srivastava presents a list of technologies that have been introduced in India for women's various activities (especially the non-productive tasks). For example, under the heading 'Shelter' are listed:

fireproof thatched rooves; waterproof mud plaster for walls; stabilized earth flooring; providing scientific ventilation and layout of household needs; improved houses for low-income groups; techniques for constructing simple hygienic latrines with septic tanks; scientific disposal of waste and used water; an improved kerosene lantern and 'deva' for smokeless lighting; construction of rural houses in seismic zones; use of ferro-cement for storing water and food-grains, cattle mangers and for roofing; use of agricultural wastes for making boards and corrugated sheets for partition walls and roofing. (Srivastava 1985: 58)

The activities carried out by women in their community management role are an extension of their reproductive activities. One task for which technology is very relevant is the supply and distribution of water. Gender and water supply and sanitation have been the subject of many recent publications. See for this the abstract journal *Woman, Water and Sanitation*, published by PROWESS/ UNDP-World Bank and the International Water and Sanitation Centre (IRC) and Hombergh (1993: 72–3). The NEDA sector paper 'Women, Water and Sanitation' gives a detailed, practical overview of the involvement of women in water and sanitation projects. Other technologically relevant tasks include sanitation, medical technologies (see Giri 1990; and IWTC 1986: 88–114) and transport, which will be discussed in Chapter 8.

To describe adequately how technology could interact with the gender needs of women in their reproductive and community management roles, it would be necessary to make an elaborate inventory of the activities that make up these roles. Such an inventory could be used to identify where technologies are used, where they are not used but could be introduced to assist gender needs, and where technological changes could redefine gender needs. Such an analysis is beyond the scope of this chapter, but some strategies can be suggested as to how technology could be introduced as a means of fulfilling gender needs.

Strategies Improved technologies could undoubtedly lighten women's tasks in their reproductive and community management roles. The aim of this strategy is to design, transfer and disseminate so-called drudgery-reducing technologies that could make life easier for women, increase their spare time, and improve their health by easing back-breaking work. This strategy has many similarities with innovation and dissemination in the context of women's enterprises, which will be discussed in Chapter 2.

As in all cases where attempts are made to achieve certain effects through technological change, it should be remembered that effects never arise from a technology itself, but always from the interplay between the technology and the complicated social, cultural and economic patterns that form its context. The outcomes of this interplay are often surprising; they can be unintended, unexpected and/or unwanted. For example, when a woman's task is made simpler by a technology, she may gain no extra free time, but other family members may simply withdraw their help. An example of this from the North is the dishwasher. Next to putting the garbage outside, dishwashing was the one household task in which it was common for a husband or a son to lend a hand (they would dry the dishes, while the wife washed them). The greatest change that the dishwasher has made to household work is that men no longer assist in the chore of washing dishes. It is important to try to predict such outcomes, in order to identify and perhaps circumvent them.

In many cases it has been found that drudgery-reducing technologies for women in their reproductive and community management roles are not adopted on a sustainable basis unless they (also) generate economic benefits (see Bargel 1990; Joss 1989), particularly if the technology is expensive to buy and/or maintain. Apparently, the increase of women's health and spare time is not a priority if it costs (too much) money. This could reflect the way women weigh different benefits, but is probably mainly an effect of the 'internal dynamics' of the household; that is, the way decision-making power is divided among the different members of the household. For this reason, Ahmed has pleaded that an economic approach is also adopted in devising technology aid for women's reproductive and community management activities (Ahmed 1985). The idea of opportunity costs, and the question of expected returns on investment, are also relevant here. For example, what can women do – or, more specifically, what can they earn – with the time they save? For example, if a woman can produce more in less time, is there a market to absorb the extra products? Are there enough raw materials? If not, should the women be encouraged to take up a new economic activity in the newly gained time?

It is now well recognized that women's various roles are not separate, but that they are intertwined with and influence each other. Many projects have adopted the dual approach of introducing drudgery-reducing technologies as well as creating opportunities that will generate incomes. For example, women have been given graters to ease their daily (reproductive) task of making gari out of cassava, and at the same time have been presented with opportunities to become (more) active in some kind of business, either in selling the extra gari produced, or in other unrelated fields. In this way, technical aid for women's reproductive and community management activities can take on an economic significance.

Conclusions

In relation to the gender needs of women in their various roles, technology has two 'faces': it can appear as a potential threat, for example in the form of competition, and as a potential ally or opportunity.

Technology is a *potential threat* when technological changes are introduced into the environments within which women perform their various roles. These technological changes can have fundamental impacts on women's gender needs; not infrequently, they are dis-empowering.

Some micro-level strategies aiming to deal with this threat have been described. However, the technical changes that are taking place around women are really part of a trend towards technical and economic expansion that is taking place at the macro-level. Thus, any micro-strategies that are adopted to counter this macro-trend are bound to have only marginal effects. One such strategy, related to the issue of the marginalization of women labourers, is to initiate *positive action programmes* at the company level, such as training to encourage the entry of women into non-traditional jobs.

Another strategy to reduce the threat of technology to women is aimed specifically at development programmes that can have an impact on the environment of women by stimulating technical change. By increasing the awareness of gender relations and of the needs of women among development workers, such issues could be better incorporated into the design of programmes or projects. In this strategy, known as *mainstreaming*, the aims and the means seem to be more balanced than in the positive action strategy, and although this strategy will certainly not be easy, it may be a feasible one.

Technology can also be seen as a *potential ally or opportunity* for

women. The aim of strategies to take advantage of this opportunity
is to develop, produce and transfer technologies to women, to help
them to expand their businesses, and to increase the efficiency of
their reproductive activities or their paid labour. These strategies,
which could be referred to as technology input strategies, are more
in line with the macro-trend towards technical and economic expansion, and thus are more likely to be effective. Sometimes, however,
they may contradict some elements of this trend, such as in instances
where the gender needs of women demand low capital investments
or even (a return to) indigenous technologies.

It is worth exploring further the ways in which technology can be
an opportunity for women to help them fulfil their gender needs.
The technology input approach has potential, and has been used in
many development programmes. There are also many complications,
however, and often the anticipated impacts have not materialized.
However, sufficient experience has been accumulated to make it
possible to discuss both the potentials and the complications of this
approach in more detail. This will be done in the next chapter,
which focuses on technology inputs to women's enterprises, although
many of the issues discussed are also relevant to technology inputs to
help women in their reproductive and community management roles.

2. Technology inputs for women's small enterprises

This chapter focuses on the potential roles of technology in the development and support of women's small enterprises. As explained in Chapter 2, tools, equipment or machines function only by virtue of the right kind of context factors. Thus, this chapter is concerned with context factors at least as much as with the tools themselves.

The chapter starts with a description of some characteristics that many women-run enterprises share. Then a short review is presented of what has been done in the field of technology and women's enterprises so far. After this, the main part of the chapter discusses the two elements that determine the effectiveness of technology innovation and transfer: the *appropriateness* of the technology and its *accessibility*. For long-term effects, both the appropriateness and the access have to be *sustainable*.

Women's enterprises

The majority of women's enterprises tend to have a number of characteristics in common. It is important to be aware of these as they influence the needs of the women who run them, as well as the effectiveness of development interventions including technology inputs.

As was described in Chapter 1, most of the enterprises owned by women are very small, and have low profit margins and little opportunity for investment. They are sometimes part-time or seasonal, and are frequently run from the home. Yet, however small they are, such enterprises are intended to provide essential financial gains to their owner and to her household, even if the gains are marginal or supplement other sources of income. And all of these businesses could profit from some kind of support. Therefore, when discussing the possibilities of improving women's business with technology inputs, no businesses are excluded from consideration beforehand. 'Small enterprises' in this chapter include those with between five and twenty-five employees (which are small enterprises according to UNIDO's definition; Keddie et al. 1988), as well as 'micro-enterprises' (up to four employees) and enterprises which are so small that some prefer to call them 'income-generating activities' (see Alkema et al. 1993). Of these, the small enterprises form 'the overwhelming majority' (Keddie et al. 1988), and women's enterprises are over-represented in that category.

The enterprises within this category still vary much with regard to their levels of investment, their capacity for the absorption of capital (including machines), the enterprising approach of their owners, the amount of time spent within the enterprise, and so on. These differences are important because they will determine which interventions will be appropriate for a given enterprise.

One characteristic of female-run enterprises is worth discussing at some length. This concerns their so-called security orientation (described, among others, by Tinker 1987; and Downing 1991). Female entrepreneurs often do not aim for growth of their enterprise in the same degree that many male entrepreneurs do. If female entrepreneurs have the opportunity for expansion, they more often diversify their activities, rather than increase their investment in one specialized activity. This is a strategy of spreading and thus minimizing risks. Women's enterprises are security-oriented, rather than growth-oriented. Stabilization of income, rather than maximization of income, is the main aim.

Women's tendency to diversify into multiple enterprises has to do with their limited access to large markets – caused among other factors by their limited mobility – and may be further stimulated by the sector in which many women work: service and trade rather than manufacturing. The security-oriented strategy is also a result of their limited access to resources and their greater responsibility for the daily subsistence of children and other family members. Perhaps most interestingly, women's security orientation is often a consequence of men's risky growth-oriented strategy; wives compensate for the risks that their husbands take, thus guaranteeing a basic income to feed the family. Likewise, the more risky investments of men are in part possible because of their wives' security orientation (Downing 1991: 6).

The conceptual shift in seeing entrepreneurs as risk-avoiding rather than profit-maximizing should not be underestimated. For example, 'objective' theories of entrepreneurial behaviour still argue that entrepreneurial behaviour is determined by rationality, where rationality is equated with 'the desire to gain the most benefit for oneself'. This is supposed to be 'identical for every person' (Muench 1995: 4). Maybe more importantly, the very idea of 'enterprising' includes associations with boldness, risk-taking, expansion and the motivation of private financial gain. As this attitude is not typical of women entrepreneurs, a definition of 'enterprise' that makes these characteristics into a *sine qua non* will not include the majority of economically active women as real entrepreneurs. Special terms are then invented for women's businesses, such as income-generating activities (Alkema et al. 1993), pre-entrepreneurial activities or survival activities (Eigen 1992: 7). In other words, the prevailing definition of a real entrepreneur tends to be gender-biased.

Most important for our purpose is that also much enterprise *support* is based on the principle that a 'real' enterprise is a growth-oriented enterprise. Many programmes will treat investment, quality improvement and expansion of market share as the logical components of any business scheme. There is a lack of enterprise support that starts from the objective of stability, or of guaranteeing flexibility and limited time-investment. There is a lack of support mechanisms that help perfect risk-spreading strategies (such as the strategy to diversify enterprises), and that promote dynamic enterprise management through means other than growth. For example, it would be useful to have a systematic analysis of when and how limited amounts of growth are possible and necessary, and how these can be achieved without compromising on risk-minimalization. In short, there is need for a stability-oriented small enterprise support (see also Everts 1995: 15).

This issue is relevant for technology support to women's enterprises. Technical improvements almost always require investments, which are usually only economically viable when production time and capacity are increased. Sometimes the technical change leads to a higher-quality product, which usually requires accessing a different, more advanced, market. This is not by definition inappropriate for small, informal, intermittently run and flexible enterprises. However, it should also not automatically be supposed that all enterprises should go into this kind of expansion. Projects that intend to introduce technology to women's enterprises should be prepared to conclude that some enterprises are better off continuing to work on the scale and for the market that they were involved in originally. At the same time, the possible role of technology as a factor in enterprise security and stability should be fully utilized.

What has been done

Since the 1970s there have been many initiatives to transfer technology to women. Technology is introduced to women's enterprises in the hope of helping them in their need for economic empowerment; it is intended to free some of their time, to broaden their economic opportunities, to break through stereotypes of women and technology as antipodes, and, most importantly, to increase their incomes. Some of these initiatives, such as the ILO project in Ghana and UNIFEM's 'WAFT' project, have been broadly set up:

- From 1980 to 1983, the ILO carried out the 'Africa Regional Project on Technical Change, Basic Needs and the Conditions of Rural Women'. Project countries were Ghana and Sierra Leone. A number of pilot activities were carried out and there were three major outputs: a manual on food-processing technologies for West Africa (ILO 1984), a volume of analytical papers (Ahmed 1985), and a summary of most important project findings (ILO and NCWD 1987). The publication edited by Iftikhar Ahmed focuses on technology transfer to rural African women, aimed at both their productive and their reproductive activities. It is one of the few publications that tries to get beyond the recounting of different case experiences, to developing some general insights that might help predict the way technological changes work out for women.
- Also in 1985, the United Nations Development Fund for Women (UNIFEM) initiated a global programme on Women and Food Technologies (WAFT) which aimed at increasing women's access

to improved food-cycle technologies. The programme included a range of pilot technology projects in the African region which focused on technology transfer and training. Available monitoring and evaluation reports and survey results have been used to strengthen UNIFEM's activities in technology transfer. Recognizing women's needs for easily accessible information on available technologies, UNIFEM produced a series of eleven food-cycle technology source books which were widely distributed to women's organizations, technology institutes, development agencies, documentation and training centres, project staff and development planners in all regions. Following the positive response to these source books, UNIFEM is now producing a second series of source books on energy and environmental technologies.

• In 1995, the United Nations Advisory Committee on Science and Technology for Development, which has had a Gender Working Group since 1993, published nine 'expert papers' on women, science and technology (Gender Working Group 1995)

Alongside these broad initiatives, myriad, often incidental, attempts have been made to help women through the provision of 'improved' tools or equipment.

Documentation on initiatives   A number of initiatives involving technology transfer to women have been documented in *Blacksmith, Baker, Roofing-sheet Maker* (Carr 1984). Although the book is not specifically about technology, but about any activity that helps women earn an income, it is interesting to see that technology is an important element in almost all of the fifty-five cases. The book is especially valuable because it provides a mix of both more and less successful cases. Many of the cases actually break through this simplistic dichotomy and show projects that have been moderately successful. Some cases from India have been described in *Women and Technology* (Jain 1985), and others from Africa are described in the volume edited by Iftikhar Ahmed (1985), some in great detail and with a systematic analysis. Other cases have been documented in journals such as *Appropriate Technology*, *Food Chain*, *ILEIA*, *African Technology Forum* and *Asia-Pacific Tech Monitor*. Many projects of technology transfer to women have been documented in internal reports or evaluations, although such information is not always easily accessible. Some case descriptions are given in journals from ITDG and AIT (e.g. IT Publications 1988; ATI 1995). Case descriptions that would be most instructive, such as those giving detailed process descriptions that honestly recount all steps and missteps in attempts at technology transfer, are not common.

Kinds of technologies   What kinds of technologies or tasks are the initiatives mostly concerned with? In *Blacksmith, Baker, Roofing-sheet Maker*, Carr tries to include cases of women involved in non-traditional activities, such as those earning money as blacksmiths, carpenters and as managers of a bus service. Overall, however, technology transfer aimed at women has mostly involved only a few domains. First of all, much attention has been paid to women's reproductive role and, within that role, the majority of work has gone into cooking stoves. Since the late 1970s, stove programmes have been started up everywhere. Many 'improved' stoves have been and are still being developed, in the hope of achieving the combined goals of lightening women's burden, reducing deforestation, and improving health and safety within the home. Within the productive role, most attention has been given to food processing, textiles and handicrafts.

This limitation to only some technologies is partly a result of Western biases as to what is seen as a woman's task. It is also partly the result of the judgement that technology transfer should deal with women's present, existing activities. Indeed, women's present activities are confined to only a few kinds. This was, for example, a consistent finding in the country papers for a broad study in the SADC countries. For instance, in Zimbabwe, 75 per cent of women's enterprises are in clothing, textiles, crochet and basket-making. Support agencies have not broken through these limitations (Carr 1993). Also in cases where attempts have been made to create *new* economic activities for women with the help of technology transfer, these new activities are usually still gender-conservative; that is, they fit within traditional expectations (of the development worker or of the recipient culture) of what is women's work.

In practice it is often wise and effective to link up with activities that women are already used to doing, and with activities that are seen as fitting for women. However, some authors argue that this range of activities needs to be broadened in order to provide women with greater opportunities for reaching viable markets (Carr 1993: 113; Ahmed 1985: 115).

'Low-tech' Another element of this dilemma is that almost all attempts at technology transfer to women involve what used to be called 'appropriate' technologies; that is, technologies that were thought to be appropriate because of their small size, their low level of complexity, their relatively low cost and their environment-friendliness. This means that the transfer of larger and more complex technologies to women has been virtually non-existent. The 'natural-ness' of regarding women's technologies as 'simple' (while transfer to men has included technologies of all levels of complexity) is worth questioning. Here again, it is true that, in practice, given the general dynamics of the informal sector (see, for example, Maldonado and Sethurantan 1992) and the small scale of most women's enterprises, low-tech technologies will often be more appropriate to women's needs than complex ones. Yet it cannot be maintained that this will *always* be so. Carr's example of a bus acquired by a group of Kenyan women illustrates that sometimes a complex technology can provide an answer to a gender need. Moreover, it is now generally recognized that even small, simple and cheap technologies, even those that utilize local materials, may sometimes not deserve to be called appropriate, in the sense that they are not perceived by the beneficiaries as an adequate answer to a particular need. Carr (1984) gives the example of a peanut oil press introduced in Burkino Faso, which showed all the right characteristics in that it was small, cheap, simple to use and locally produced. However, it replaced the least demanding step in the oil-making process (bringing the peanuts to the local mill to be ground for a small fee, adding boiling water to them and skimming off the oil). It took four times as long to do this. Moreover, with the new machine it was no longer possible to make the by-product of the traditional process: the peanut cookies which in fact gave more profit than the oil itself (Carr 1984: 22–3).

For this reason, the term 'appropriate' technology is a confusing one. It cannot be used to describe characteristics of a technology in itself, it only describes a relation between a technology and its bene-ficiaries (see also Veken and Hernandez 1986: 8; Anderson 1985: 68).

Prototypes versus dissemination Possibly hundreds of technologies have been developed world-wide to assist women in their traditional productive work or to expand their productive activities. To give just a few examples, new technologies have been described for: carpet weaving, basket making, oil pressing, soap making, cassava grating, gari processing, beer brewing, pottery, coir work, silk reeling, milling of peanuts and different kinds of grains, food preservation, rice threshing and winnowing, and cracking of palm kernels. The tools have often been developed within technology institutes that specialize in small, simple and low-cost technologies. It seems quite possible to get such organizations, even though they are almost all dominated by male personnel, to work for women, that is, to design technologies that are intended to be used in tasks traditionally done by women. It may even be true that, on the 'low-tech' level, just as many innovations are made for what are traditionally women's tasks as are made for men's traditional tasks. As said before, the idea that the best technology might be low-tech rather than high-tech seems to be more readily accepted when the envisioned beneficiaries are women rather than men. Certainly, many low-tech innovations are in the food-processing sector, where women are the dominant producers. For example, in the West African technology institutes studied by the ILO, the large majority of the technologies developed are for traditional women's work (ILO 1984: 244–5). (On the other hand, in Kogi et al.'s (1989) study, *Low-cost Ways of Improving Working Conditions: 100 Examples from Asia*, only one of the 100 examples describes a job in which women are employed.) However, there is a catch here: what is a female task *before* an improved technology is adopted, sometimes becomes a male task afterwards.

It is becoming increasingly clear that the bottleneck in technology transfer is to be found not in the development of prototypes, but in the sustainable dissemination of the technology. Many of the ideas that have been developed in AT institutes around the world have a hard time leaving the workshop and reaching the intended beneficiaries. This is true in general (Darrow et al. 1981), but certainly for the technologies for women too. On the other hand, some technologies do spread quickly. Examples cited in an informal overview by UNIFEM (1990a) include the Chorkor fish-smoking oven in Ghana and the improved *jiko* (charcoal stove) in Kenya. The essential elements in dissemination are appropriateness, access and sustainability.

The issue of appropriateness

Inappropriateness is very often the main reason for disappointing results with technology transfer. There are many aspects of a technology that need to be appropriate, and a shortcoming in just one of these aspects can be enough to make a technology project fail.

Documentation on appropriateness In the documentation on cases mentioned above, the reasons for the problems or failures of technology transfer, where these are mentioned, often sound familiar; they confirm the lists of what to be aware of when designing and transferring technology (e.g. Carr 1985; Carr's chapter in Ahmed 1985; Veken and Hernandez 1988; ILO and NCWD 1985). The interesting conclusion can be drawn that, by and large, many of the reasons for failure through inappropriateness have been well described. Failure seldom occurs for unexpected reasons.

There are some areas in which the written information on appropriateness could be improved.

• The information could be better organized and presented more systematically in order to make it easier to remember and apply. The following paragraph gives one such checklist of factors of appropriateness:
• Some subjects, such as basic business economics, could be given greater emphasis. According to Zoomers (1993: 22), appropriateness is not only 'adapting to the local environment' (i.e. bringing technology in line with the available resources, local habits, needs and human resource capacities), but should also be appropriate from the business point of view. Too often, plans to introduce 'improved' technologies to small enterprises do not include basic calculations of the required level of investment, returns on investment and break-even points. Such basic calculations would show, for example, how much profit will be required on a regular basis in order to repay the investment. Given the costs and current market prices, this requires a certain level of turnover, which again presupposes the availability of a supply of raw materials, labour, time and, of course, a market for the increased production. With very small enterprises, often the conclusion of such a calculation can only be that such an investment is not warranted, given the

market and business opportunities and constraints of the enterprise. In general, when all the factors of appropriateness are
considered seriously, one must be prepared to decide more often
than has been done in the past, that in a given situation technology
may *not* be an appropriate answer to women's need for economic
empowerment. This issue is one of the somewhat controversial
points stressed in the training on introducing technology to
women's enterprises which is described in Chapter 3.

• More '*how-to*' information regarding the appropriateness of
technology design is needed. By this is meant information that
not only indicates the factors to be aware of, but also gives guidelines on how to gather the necessary information about these
factors, on how this information can be translated into practice,
and how to make the correct judgements. The 'how-to' aspect of
appropriateness is discussed below.

In spite of such possible improvements it seems that the production
of better information about effective technology transfer is not the
main bottleneck. Thus it is questionable whether better information
alone would provide the full solution to improving the effectiveness
of technical support to women's enterprises. It is at this time more
useful to encourage intermediate organizations and development
workers to read existing publications (more carefully). *Training programmes* such as those described in Chapter 3 could stimulate this,
and could also help development workers to put the information into
practice. Other bottlenecks are discussed below.

The factors of appropriateness   Different lists of the factors or
dimensions that together make up the appropriateness of a technological 'improvement' can be constructed, and in fact they have been
constructed by different authors (e.g. Carr 1985; Carr's chapter in
Ahmed 1985; Veken and Hernandez 1988; ILO and NCWD 1985).
Veken and Hernandez (1988) describe three kinds of appropriateness:
technical, socio-cultural and socio-economic appropriateness. Socio-
cultural appropriateness includes appropriateness in relation to family
systems, religion, division of labour, training and education, control
of income, and forms of organization. All such elements could be
called the 'factors of appropriateness'; that is, those aspects (factors)
for which we should ask ourselves whether the technology is

appropriate, perhaps using a checklist. Anderson (1985) does not list what to be aware of when attempting to introduce a technology, but provides an inventory of the ways in which technology can *affect* women. This is in fact another side of the same coin.

By integrating these lists and combining them with information on reasons for success and failure from other publications and project reports, the author developed a list of twenty-three factors that summarize the main reasons for failures or conditions for success of technology transfer. In this list, the factors are divided into the following categories:

- Assessing the need (factors include: problems experienced and their causes, involvement of women and men).
- A business approach (factors include: market situation, supply situation, business training).
- Necessary provisions (factors include: organizing the production, credit provision).
- What is the best technical option? (factors include: size of technical step, requirements for operation, technical soundness and durability, repair facilities).
- (Un)intended effects (factors include: effects of the technology on the mechanized activity, effects of the technology on linked activities).
- The wider context (factors include social-cultural constraints, economic macro-environment, political environment).

The full list of factors appears in the Appendix. Some of the factors are illustrated with cases from Ghanaian development workers who participated in a training programme on these factors.

'How-to' information: how to judge what is appropriate
What can be said about *how to* improve the appropriateness of technology, about the methods and practice of this endeavour? The degree of appropriateness of a technology cannot be inferred from its size, level of complexity or from any other characteristic of the technology *per se*. Appropriateness is a characteristic of the relationship between a technology, the environment and its purpose; it cannot be created in the laboratory. Any method for creating or judging appropriateness must therefore include some kind of confrontation between the technology on the one hand, and the user

and the user's context on the other. The three elements of this confrontation are: (1) the use of baseline data and feasibility studies; (2) participation or (other) consumer linkages; and (3) an iterative process.

1. *Use of baseline data and feasibility studies* Since appropriateness means that technology fits within a context, it is clear that there must be information about the situation within which the technology is to function. Not only must the needs of the women be known, but also a much broader range of information on resources and circumstances. According to a recent evaluation of UNIFEM's gender and technology projects to date: 'Projects from Africa that were formulated with clear insight into women's existing skills, knowledge and needs significantly facilitated the introduction and use of technology and credit.' A series of examples illustrates this:

> In Togo, fish smokers readily adopted the new fish smoking technology as it fitted in with their occupation and capabilities, and they were highly motivated. The Togo project built on the fact that the women already had a trade union and had found that working in groups was advantageous. [...] In the Kenyan Karachuonyo Women's Pottery project, the feasibility study was undertaken too late to establish that the water and fuel needed to operate the kiln were not available, and that the roads were inadequate for distribution of the pottery. [...] Understanding women's leadership structures and women's role in informal and formal decision-making enabled the Ghana Federation of Business and Professional Women to build on this as a means of ensuring that the project had the desirable impact and provided women ownership of its activities. (UNIFEM 1994: 3–5)

Moreover, such an assessment of needs and feasibility has to be thorough; in a recent evaluation study of twelve technology projects for women in Ghana, it was concluded that it is not enough to do just a short survey (Baffour-Awuah and Minnow-Hagan 1994). Good guidelines on how to collect adequate baseline data, and methodologies for conducting resource analyses and needs assessments are available, yet some technology projects are still not based on adequate data and feasibility studies.

2. *Participation or (other) consumer linkages* Since the 1970s it has frequently been stressed that technologies should be designed through a participatory process. As it became clear that development workers were often not reaching their target groups, 'participation' became a popular creed. Many different things are meant by participation (see Moser 1993: 100–4). In the context of improved technologies, the main point is that appropriateness can be proven only in practice. Therefore the confrontations with this practice (for example try-outs) must intertwine with technology design or choice. There could be many different forms of such 'confrontations' (or, less polemical: interactions). Forms of consumer 'participation' actually take place in most professional R&D processes, even (or rather particularly) in the development of 'high-tech'. Examples of such interactions, including consumer research, laboratory experiments with potential users, try-outs of prototypes by volunteers, and even the 'hit-and-miss' strategy of 'throwing a product on the market', can be seen as confrontations with the intended beneficiaries.

The process of 'sitting down with the women' and letting them discover the technological improvements they need, is only one form of participatory development. This may be one of the more em- powering ones for women, but it has the disadvantage that it is very time-consuming, both for the extension workers and also for the women themselves. Moreover, to ask women to participate even in the technology *design* ignores the reasons for the division of labour between producers and users of tools, such as the differences in technical education. But even if technology *design* is not included in the participation process, it remains a labour-intensive and time- consuming process:

> Experiences over the past five years have led to the following two major conclusions: first the extension approach to technology dissemination is a very long-term affair. For example, in Lesotho, it has taken the WAFT Project two years to introduce improved technologies to women in one village and to train one local extension worker. [...] Either the extension route needs to be made more efficient and/or a more market-oriented approach needs to be taken. (UNIFEM 1990c: 2)

The desire for greater effectiveness expressed in the above extract is understandable, and indeed a shorter time-frame than the two years of the Lesotho example may in many cases be attempted. But in general, finding or designing a technology that is appropriate given the very small sizes of many women's enterprises, the resources of their area, the gender-related constraints of their lives and so on, cannot be done quickly. More haste will usually be less speed.

What about the potential of more market-oriented approaches? What market-based mechanisms could help to channel women's voices and needs in order to influence the technology design process? Market-based linkages can in some cases be a less labour-intensive form of user participation. In a way, rural grassroots women already have some power as 'consumers' of development projects: if they reject a technology, the project fails. However, unlike a business, which would lose profits or go bankrupt in such a case, a development project usually does not feel the consequences of women's rejection 'in its pocket'. Women's power would be increased if it did.

Of course, women's power as consumers is limited because most of them have little direct purchasing power. Yet with the subsidies given to projects for poor women, they do have a form of indirect purchasing power. Market-driven forms of technology promotion use and strengthen this consumer power so that it can become a force that ensures that women's needs are met. Chapter 4 will look further into issues surrounding the involvement of women in market-driven ways to promote technology.

3. *Iterative process*   One last point on *how to* achieve appropriateness is that it can never be achieved 'beforehand', that is, before the technology leaves the lab. Carr (1984) illustrates this point in each of the cases she describes, in which there is a going back and forth of near failures and corrections (just as in any other enterprise). A banana chips project in Papua New Guinea provides a good example.

A nearby technology centre assisted village women in developing the idea of making banana chips and taught women how to do it. When the kerosene stove which the women used was found to be too expensive, the centre taught the villagers how to build a wood-efficient stove. Later again, it intervened when the banana chip production was almost closed down by the health authorities. The centre taught the women how to modify their equipment and handling so that their production unit would comply with health regulations (Carr 1984: 41–2).

In this case the road to an appropriate technology had at least three major loops. The problems were solvable when they arose, but probably could not have been dealt with at the start of the project.

Whether we are talking about the development of an improved tool, or about the *selection* of the best available tool, in most cases finding an appropriate technology is an iterative process.

Barriers to appropriateness Although some points could be given greater emphasis in guidelines on technology transfer, in general the available publications offer much practical and basic information and advice. Nevertheless, 'still the mistakes are made over and over again' (Carr in the Foreword to Luery et al. 1992). I will discuss some possible reasons for this.

Performance indicators Some institutional factors make it difficult to achieve appropriateness, in spite of the good advice given in many publications. One factor may be the pressure to perform within a limited time period. Many sponsors demand tangible results. Prototypes for a new technology are very tangible and relatively easy to develop, since (to put it somewhat crudely) it is necessary to come to terms only with the physical laws of nature, and not with the laws of culture, politics, psychology, economics, etc. Thus, in some cases there may be a reward for quickly developing new prototypes, rather than going through the laborious process of field testing, discussions with beneficiaries and redesign, organizing access and promoting sustainability. Likewise, for organizations working on the dissemination of tools, there may be too great an emphasis on 'input indicators' for measuring the success of technology transfer, rather than 'output indicators'. For example, an input indicator could be the number of machines that are brought *into* a village; an output indicator might be the number of women who after two years have increased their earnings *out of* using the machine. In general, there seems to be a lack of incentives (either positive or negative) for development workers to adopt the rather labour-intensive methodology that is a requirement for effectiveness. Indeed, some sort of 'culture-change' among development workers may be required in order to bridge the gap between general knowledge of the factors of appropriateness, and applying this in daily practice.

Thus, with regard to technology transfer, donors should avoid pressuring agents into the short-term production of prototypes. Rather, they should pressure for long-term performance with regard to appropriateness and sustainability. Donor agents might be more willing to do this if better indicators were devised for measuring progress along this much less tangible route.

Technology institutes and dissemination There is another institutional barrier to integrating existing knowledge on appropriateness into the practice of technology design. As discussed above, methodologies for making technology appropriate must include at least some form of contact with the intended beneficiaries. Institutes for technology design are not always well placed for this, for a number of reasons. In a literal sense they are often far removed from the villages where the technology is to live its life in the future. Technology centres may, for example, be linked to a university and situated on campus, from where it is not easy to interact with poor rural or urban grassroots women.

More importantly, it is not always part of the tradition of technology institutes to keep in contact with the intended beneficiaries. This may be because those working at the institutes are predominantly technically rather than socially oriented. For example, of the ten West African technology institutes studied by the ILO in 1984, none employed in-house social scientists, and 'identification of areas for design and development in no case involved socio-economic studies' (ILO 1984). Some institutes explicitly concentrate on prototype design and leave the dissemination to other parties. This makes it impossible to make the dissemination process part of the design process; in other words, to make the achievement of appropriateness an iterative process.

Thus, it would be a positive change if, for each incipient technology, more interaction could be organized between the technology institutes and the user context. As discussed above, the best form of interactive technology design is not always 'sitting down with the women'. Other, more market-oriented methods would require much less extension work by technology designers themselves. One of the current challenges is to create and support market mechanisms that help fulfil gender needs. It is questionable whether (subsidized) technology centres should remain key actors in this. According to UNIFEM:

Recent work sponsored by ITDG in Africa and elsewhere reveals that the most useful source of technology for small farmers and entrepreneurs is the informal sector, and that innovation takes place here as a spontaneous two-way process between the artisan and his [*sic*] clients. Statistics demonstrate that almost 80% of innovations to cassava graters in Benin State were made by artisans in direct response to women users. It seems likely that grassroots women are already far closer to artisans than they will ever get to University level technologists, and that rapid progress could be made by encouraging these linkages. (UNIFEM 1990c: 16)

While this may be true in general, it should be remembered that the traditional relations between artisans and potential customers in many cases also need to be improved, in order to increase the customers' influence on the producers.

Gender issues within institutions If it is difficult for technology centres to reach the people, is it even more difficult for them to reach the women among the people? The fact that technology institutes are predominantly male domains suggests that it would be. For example, in many cultures it is difficult for men to come into contact with women, and, because of their very different everyday worlds, it may be difficult for men to imagine the needs and situations of women. This gender barrier to understanding needs is quite similar to those presented by class and cultural differences. Such barriers can be overcome; good research, using appropriate methods and intermediaries, will help to transfer information from poor to rich, from women to men, from rural to urban, when combined with an open mind and a genuine interest. Not that it will be easy:

> How do we know whether a target group in a village or region really gives priority to the planned activities? When the project staff go to a village with a hypodermic or with needle and thread, women spontaneously ask for medical assistance and sewing courses. Whether this request meets their real needs, is not certain. Women are not used to being interviewed about their needs and motivations. It will take time before they can formulate their problems. (Veken and Hernandez 1988: 105)

So far, the organizations that have most experience with and are most effective in reaching women are women's organizations (Carr 1993). Thus the time may not be ripe to integrate all activities which specifically target women, into 'general' organizations. An alternative would be to set up 'women's desks' or 'women's windows' within general organizations.

The issue of accessibility

Sometimes tools may be appropriate to women's gender needs, yet women may not be able to access them. They may not know of them (information); they may not be able to afford them (financing); they may not know how to use them (training); improved access may require new forms of organizing the production (organization); and/or the technology may not be easily available because of inadequate production and distribution channels (availability). These five factors are discussed below.

Information What kind of information on technologies could be of use to women (or to the extension workers working directly with women)? Three possible goals of information can be distinguished, each of which is a little more comprehensive than the one before.

Goal 1: Women gain a general acquaintance with the existence of certain 'improved' tools.
Goal 2: Women know how to judge the usefulness of different technical options.
Goal 3: Women can make final choices among the options available.

These are all goals or objectives relating to the consumer; that is, the (potential) user of the technology (such as the woman who produces and sells fruit juice). Information for technology users should not be confused with information for technology *producers*. Only a few improved technologies are so simple that the users can also be producers and only one kind of information is required. For example: the technical solution for keeping crawling bugs and ants out of food is to place the legs of the chest or table in saucers of water; again, the so-called 'Dixy bag' is an invention that makes it possible to pick small fruit or beans with two hands while the picked fruits fall directly into the bag. The bag is attached to one hand, with fingers sticking through it, and it is held open by a piece of wire. (The latter technology is described in Centre of Science for Villages 1986: 129.)

Usually, a division of labour between users and producers is the only practical way to organize technology transfer. In these cases, only the information for producers needs to include detailed instructions on how to build the machine or tool. Consumers need information that enables them to find out which technological options are appropriate for them, and how to access these.

1. *General acquaintance* A number of books seem to be adequate for this purpose. They include source books (anthologies or compendia) that cover a wide range of activities and present a broad overview of (simple) tools from all continents. These books can give women a general knowledge of the kinds of tools that exist and that might be useful to them. By looking through a general source book, women can broaden their technical horizons and may become interested in some of the tools shown.

On the other hand, given the broad range of tools and the many different situations in which women live, many of the tools will not be applicable to an individual reader. This drawback could be reduced if source books were written for specific groups of users (for example, rural women in desert areas, or urban slum women without access to electricity, and so on). To my knowledge, such general source books for specific groups do not yet exist.

The books that fall into this category of offering general acquaintance (e.g. Centre of Science for Villages 1986; IWTC 1986) often include cartoon-like drawings to make them more accessible to grassroots women. Contrary to the distinction between information for users and for producers of technology, some of these books do contain technical construction drawings, although usually not detailed enough for a tool maker to work from. Yet such drawings do seem to suggest that anyone should be able to make these tools for themselves, which may discourage some readers. Moreover, the technical drawings do little to help women to acquaint themselves with the tool. It is not necessary to understand the technical principles, if the reader's purpose is to get a general idea of what a tool is about.

Although these books are written in simple language, they are usually in English. Books are not an ideal means of communication, since in many cultures there is not a strong tradition of reading, even when the beneficiaries are literate and understand English. Thus, tool fairs and travelling demonstrations should also be considered as ways of enabling women to get hands-on experience with the tools. Media such as radio, television and movies or theatre could also help in providing a basic acquaintance.

In general, however, the practical relevance of this first goal may be limited. Since the applicability and availability of tools vary widely even within a region, general information is of limited practical use in a particular village or town. To apply the technical suggestions will often require the intervention of an institution that can import, test and adjust the tools.

2. *Knowing how to make a judgement* The second goal that can be supported by information is to supply women with background knowledge that can help them judge what kind of technical 'improvements' would or would not be useful for them. As in the first case, it is not necessary to present all the details about a specific issue and all the technologies that are available in the region; but if the aim is to offer more than a general acquaintance, then there must be a discussion of the factors that need to be considered when judging whether a technology would be useful. What technical variations need to be considered, and how are these variations relevant in different circumstances? For such an overview to be useful to women in many different circumstances, it should specifically and systematically discuss the effects of such circumstances.

This kind of overview would not be detailed enough (not up-to-date and town-specific enough) to enable women to make definitive choices, but it would help them to become better-informed and empowered partners in discussions with technology suppliers (development workers as well as firms). The UNIFEM series on food technologies is an example of information aiming at such an objective. The books are in great demand; they apparently fulfil a need.

3. *Enabling choices* The goal of enabling women to make choices between the different technological options that are available (including traditional technologies) is a very important one, but the most difficult. This ability to choose would contribute to forming a market-based linkage between users and producers, as discussed above; it is the kind of information needed to promote consumer 'participation' in technology design. Such information would eventually strengthen the position of women as technology consumers, and could provide an incentive for the design of more appropriate and better-quality technologies.

Information that would contribute to this goal can deal with only a limited number of activities or services and present possible technical solutions. The information would have to be specific, and ideally include details on the availability of the alternatives within the region, on the reputation of different suppliers and technical trainers, and so on. Also, information that aims to help women make informed consumer choices cannot be provided just once; the necessary level of detail is such that it would soon be outdated. One option is a local newsletter, recounting experiences with tools, projects, credit programmes or repair services. Non-written information would be ideal for this goal; indeed, information transmitted by word of mouth already fulfils this function to some degree. Organized household-to-household exchange is one of the most effective methods of transferring information with direct local relevance. So far, however, the flow of real consumer-supporting information towards women appears to have been rather limited.

Financing That there is a need for some kind of financing system to accompany technology transfer is now widely accepted. Even improved technologies that are economically appropriate, in the sense that they pay back their costs, are often inaccessible to women because they lack the capital to buy them. Therefore, any technology transfer programme should specifically include the credit dimension, either by including credit in the programme, or by organizing linkages with existing credit schemes. The specific needs of and barriers to women obtaining credit have been well documented (see Chen 1996; Almeyda 1996; Pruyne 1993; Hilhorst and Oppenoorth 1992) and are starting to become well known. There is a broad literature on this subject. Ordinary credit programmes still find it difficult to reach women, but there has been an increase in the number of successful credit programmes specifically for women (in particular those following the Grameen Bank formula).

However, there is a difference between credit provided for working capital and for investment in machinery, in that the payback rate for the latter is generally lower. The probable causes of this are: the amounts loaned are much higher, and the debtors are often groups. Often, loans for machines have not been paid back and development organizations have not insisted, so that in many regions women regard the machines as gifts rather than loans; and (as discussed above) quite often no adequate calculations have been made as to whether the loans *can* be paid back, even if all goes well. Unfortunately, much of the time, all does *not* go well, because one or more of the many factors of appropriateness have not been properly considered.

Training The intended beneficiaries of a new technology should of course be trained in its use, as in the following example.

In a project from the Self-Employed Women's Association's (SEWA) Rural Wing, the needs of women salt farmers were identified. These women collect salt in the desert regions in west Gujarat, India. They suffer, among other things, from fungus and cuts on their feet because they are constantly standing barefoot in saline water. Rubber boots, which may in this context be seen as a technology, were introduced. The women had to be trained in their use (Nanavaty and Buch 1990).

Usually some training in maintenance and repairs should be included, although repairs do not always need to be done in the village itself. The question of what is most realistic will depend on the availability of spare parts and repair facilities in the village, versus the accessibility of a mechanic elsewhere.

In many countries, for example in Ghana, training in operation and maintenance is usually provided by the firms that produce the equipment, and so is given not by a trainer but by an engineer. The training courses are usually very short (often only one day or a few hours), and are rarely followed up. In projects where equipment is brought to women's groups, the trainees are often also women. Yet this has rarely been effective. In almost all the groups studied in Ghana, it was found that after some time the machine will be operated by a man (Baffour-Awuah and Minnow-Hagan 1994). Breaking through this gender-based division of tasks will require a much greater effort than short technical training courses alone. It is, however, debatable whether this objective should be given priority. The solution chosen by many women's groups – to employ men to run and maintain the machines – may be an appropriate one, given the unattractiveness of the task and the already busy schedules of the women. A better focus may be to train women to know enough about the technology to be able to check what the operator does, for this is often a problem, and sometimes women are cheated by their employees. Thus 'control' is the relevant issue, rather than the act of 'operating' itself.

Training in how to deal with all the new aspects of entre-preneurship that come with a new technology is just as important. Foremost in this is marketing, since almost all tools are meant to increase either production or quality. To pay off the investment, this increased production or quality must be sold. The following case, observed in India, is typical.

A machine for leaf-plate making was developed to replace the traditional process in which plates were made by stitching leaves by hand. Rural women produced these plates for the local market of their own village. The new plates were better in quality (watertight) and could be produced around twenty times as quickly. Moreover, the machines were very simple to use. A few machines were installed in one village and the women were trained how to use them. How-ever, when they started to produce the new plates, they soon found that there was no market in their village for watertight plates if these were even the least bit more expensive. There was also no market for the greatly increased quantity of plates. Since the women had no idea how to go about finding other markets, and since they were not given any help with this, they abandoned the machines as soon as they showed some problems or when money was asked for them (personal observation, March 1994, Ahmedabad, India).

Organization of the production   Support for smaller women's enterprises is often combined with attempts to organize women into co-operatives. There can be many reasons for this. One of them is to strengthen women's bargaining power *vis-à-vis*, for example, government, suppliers of raw materials or buyers of the finished product (SEWA 1988). Through a co-operative, women can sometimes profit from economies of scale by buying raw materials in bulk and organizing transport together to the market. However, a co-operative has its own problems. For example, there may be an unavoidable tension between competition and co-operation, when the members are in fact also each other's competitors. Within development work, the co-operative has lost much of its appeal because of these prob-lems: 'UNIFEM's experience shows that group-owned enterprises are less successful than individually owned ones' (UNIFEM 1990c: 17).

When it comes to technology, however, the need to organize women into somewhat larger groups is often unavoidable because of the characteristics of the technology. Often, the new technology will be too expensive for individual women. Even if ample credit is provided and if one woman is willing to take out a large loan, then it is unlikely that she will be able to pay off the loan if the machine is not used full-time; as noted above, most women are unable to work on their enterprise full-time, and even if they do, they are unlikely to work with the machine all the time. Ideally, if a machine is bought by a group of women, it could be used continuously and thus be profited from more extensively. Thus, in most cases, group formation is the solution chosen, adding the common difficulties of group enterprises to the already difficult endeavour of providing technical support for women's enterprises. For example, in the case of a machine bought by a group, individual members may not take responsibility for its maintenance.

There are many accounts of the advantages and disadvantages of forming groups for technology transfer. This has to do with the fact that there are also many different kinds of groups. Experience in Ghana seems to show that a group is likely to be more successful when its main economic function is the management of the technology, while the production itself (rice milling, oil extraction with an improved oil press) is done by the women individually, for their own gain. Individual women may pay a fee for the use of the machine, and from this money, ideally, the machine is paid for, maintained, repaired and eventually replaced.

Another factor that determines whether a group will be successful is its size. If the formation of a co-operative is not seen as a purpose in itself, but as a means to make the introduction of a machine possible, then it is logical that the group should be as small as is necessary in order to receive the credit. Smaller groups usually function better, and can rent out the machine to non-group members.

In spite of the difficulties and valid warnings, it is too early to conclude that groups do not work. Since co-operatives sometimes work out differently for women than for men, women's co-operatives may succeed where men's co-operatives fail (and vice versa). When a co-operative fails, this may not have to do with the form of the co-operative; it may simply be the result of an untenable business idea that would also have failed as a private enterprise. Also, in the

Netherlands, 80 per cent of starting small businesses fail within two years!

Nevertheless, it is good to consider other ways of dealing with the problem of scale when introducing technologies. In another organizational form that increases the functioning time of the machine, the machine is privately exploited by one person, who asks a fee for its use. In publications on women and technology, this is sometimes presented as a regrettable development, especially if the machine owner happens to be a man (which is usually the case). The argument is that women are still not in control of the technology. Although this is true, this need not be a serious disadvantage. The woman may still be in control of the *service* provided by the machine. If the working of the market keeps prices at a reasonable level, this arrangement may certainly provide for women's gender needs. Yet if a woman is the exploiter of the machine, this will not only provide an income for her, but may in a more abstract and indirect way fulfil a strategic gender need. To accomplish this takes quite some dedication; it is necessary to break through the traditional prejudice (which exists in both rich and poor countries) that a technology must be operated by men.

Availability Access to a technology is of course dependent on its availability: it must be produced in large enough quantities to meet demand. This is often a real bottleneck in the transfer and dissemination of technologies. The ILO (1984) discussed this issue extensively and concluded that there is a 'missing link' between technology centres and small-scale industries. Only if technology centres had their own workshops were some prototypes produced. Of the eighty technologies designed in the institutes studied, only seven were produced in quantities of more than twenty per year. 'In none of the countries was there evidence of wide-scale manufacture of equipment designed and developed within countries' (ILO 1984: 246). The idea that small industries can and will simply copy a prototype for commercial production is unrealistic. Also, not all small industries can work from technical drawings. Thus, to create a linkage between those wanting to disseminate a technology and the local industrial sector may mean that training is needed for the latter. If production is taken up, ideally mechanisms of supply and demand would start to take over some of the labour-intensive extension activities. This presupposes that there is a demand among women users, which implies that small loans must be available to them, so that their need also becomes a buyer's demand.

When production becomes decentralized and starts to scale up, quality control becomes an issue, as was the case with TOOL's spinning wheel. After extensive field tests, redesign and minor corrections, the Medleri Charkha, a foot-operated spinning wheel, was found appropriate enough to be produced on a larger scale. After some searching, a local manufacturer was found who wanted to take the product on. Availability of materials was no problem, since the spinning wheel is made of locally available materials only. However, when, as a result of the growing demand, the number of charkhas produced increased from 40 to 748 a year in two years, it was difficult to keep up standards of quality. In this case, the wife of the producer was trained in spinning in order to be able to check the spin quality of the charkhas before they left the workshop, but this was only one of the aspects of the required quality control. The TOOL consultant drafted a checklist for the manufacturer, enabling him to control the quality of the different parts. However, quality control remains a source of concern (TOOL 1994: 13).

Having looked at the users of technology, we should now now consider the *producers* of technology. Here as well, gender issues abound. Why are there so few women in the production sector? Since we talk about technologies to be used by women, women might be more effective in marketing them. More importantly, women should be encouraged and trained to enter into businesses that promise to be profitable, perhaps including the production of the newly designed technologies. In this way the backward and forward linkages of technology transfer projects can address women's gender needs.

Sustainability

The introduction of a technology does not occur at one point in time. Some new, ongoing dynamic must develop in order for a technology to spread, be kept up and renewed; that is, for its intended changes and effects to be sustained. When the initial inputs, initiatives and funding are (gradually) withdrawn, a situation or system that can continue must remain. The crucial importance of sustainability is increasingly being recognized. It is discussed here as a third main element that determines the effectiveness of technology innovation and transfer (next to appropriateness and accessibility); both the appropriateness of the technical improvements and the access of women to these improvements must be sustainable.

Sustainability demands interventions and effects of a kind different from those discussed so far. Where appropriateness and accessibility can be managed through careful action and monitoring by the agents of intervention, sustainability requires mechanisms to be created that 'work by themselves'.

There is some disagreement as to what can be called sustainable. Is something sustainable when no intervention from *foreign* donors is required for it to continue? What about inputs from *local* development institutes? What if the government takes over the support of a programme (for example, to provide continuous subsidies for wood-saving ovens in order to keep their price low); does that mean that sustainability has not been achieved? Can long-term government commitment be considered a basis for a sustainability? Or are only market-driven mechanisms 'real' bases?

Sustainability adds the dimension of time to all the aspects addressed so far. When a technology is appropriate, the sustainability issue is that it *remains* appropriate. So when the economic appropriateness of a technology is dependent on access to a market, then a technology is *sustainably* appropriate only if the entrepreneurs are still able to access this market when the project staff withdraw. It is even more sustainable if the entrepreneurs have learned how to access new markets, in case the present market becomes inaccessible.

If access requires information, sustainable access requires an institute or other organizational channel that continues to produce and disseminate such information. If the design of appropriate technologies presupposes gender awareness within mainstream technology organizations, then, to ensure that technologies will also be designed appropriately in the future, we require a sustainable system for renewing and sustaining gender awareness in technology organizations. We can also see availability of repair facilities and spare parts as a sustainability issue, because it is the time dimension to the aspect of functional appropriateness (that is, whether the machine functions or not).

It is clear that sustainability is difficult to accomplish. It requires an extreme form of 'heterogeneous engineering', that is, engineering and managing a very varied set of circumstances and processes.

Conclusions

Technology is introduced to women's enterprises in the hope of helping them achieve economic empowerment. Experience shows that this is not easy, however. The chosen technology needs to be both appropriate and accessible, and must continue to be so over time, after the interventionists leave; that is, it must be sustainable. Whether a technology is 'appropriate' for increasing a woman's income through her enterprise depends on many aspects, which are called the 'factors of appropriateness'. Only some of these factors have to do with the 'hardware' of a technology. The effects and the functioning of a technology are just as dependent on the surroundings (the context) of the hardware as on the hardware itself.

Next to the factors of appropriateness (and sustainability), the various factors that influence the *accessibility* of technologies should be addressed. These include: information for women on technologies and on technical choice; financing and credit; technical and business training; and ways of organizing production around the new machine (including the formation of groups or co-operative enterprises). Finally, the local production of machines and tools must be encouraged in order to ensure that they are available to meet the demand.

There are a few publications that try to list the factors of appropriateness. I have combined these into a list of twenty-three factors. It is unlikely, however, that the publication of such a list by itself can improve the quality of technology transfer projects for women. For one thing, additional guidelines are needed that explain as clearly as possible *how to* explore each of the factors. Second, just as important as the contents of the guidelines is that they should be firmly embedded in (training) programmes that make a strong appeal to the participants to use the knowledge in practice. Such a training programme is described in the next chapter.

The discussion above also identifies a number of other measures that can improve the effectiveness of technology introduction to women. Incentives and progress indicators that reward output rather than input could stimulate the use of more effective methods of technology transfer. Also, the linkages between the producers and users of technologies, which are essential in creating appropriateness, should be strengthened. Technology institutes do not always easily maintain links with women users; a necessary alternative is to use market-based linkages. This is related to the question of what information is and could be provided to users; when women are able to choose between firms, and can exchange information on these firms, they can become a more influential market force. With regard to institutional requirements, organizations that work specifically for women are for the moment indispensable, although all general organizations should and could be made more aware of the issues involved in reaching women and in addressing women's gender needs.

3. Training in women and technology

In many countries, attempts to introduce technology to women's enterprises tend to be less effective than they should be. The introduction of new technology may actually be one of the main stumbling blocks in women's enterprise support. Yet, as was shown in Chapter 2, the main reasons for failure and preconditions for success are known and have been described in a number of publications. What is more, many local project staff members are also quite aware of these preconditions. What is needed at this point, then, is for this knowledge to be applied into effective strategies for project planning and implementation, and actually to be put into practice. Intermediate organizations involved in the introduction of technology to women must be reminded and inspired to do so, in spite of the extra investment in effort and time that this usually requires. A number of approaches could contribute to this. One important contribution can be made by a training programme specifically designed for staff of intermediate organizations.

This chapter describes the training that TOOLConsult designed, as part of the project on Gender, Technology and Economic Empowerment, which aims to enhance the effectiveness of intermediate organizations in their attempts to introduce technology to women's enterprises.

Background of the training course

The training 'Introducing Technology to Women's Enterprises' was developed by the author on the basis of the insights described in Chapter 2. It was also informed by some studies undertaken in

Ghana, the country for which the training was first designed and where it was tested. These studies included:

- A mission by the author to Ghana in 1994, in which some of the main problems and training needs were identified.[1]
- A study by D. Baffour-Awuah and F. Minnow-Hagan (1994), financed by the FIT programme (an ILO/TOOLConsult programme aimed at improving Farm Implements and Tools as well as food-processing devices).
- A Consultative Workshop in Accra on the provision of food-processing equipment to women, also organized by FIT, where this theme was discussed by some twenty-five experts.

From these studies, it was concluded that many organizations in Ghana are involved in the transfer of equipment to women, but that the effectiveness of these attempts to meet women's needs through technology transfer can be improved. The study by Baffour-Awuah and Minnow-Hagan (1994), for example, shows that in only three out of the eleven groups evaluated were the machines which had been provided or sold on credit still operative. Reasons for not producing with the machines included no market (3), not enough raw material (2) and machine breakdown (3).

Second, here again it was confirmed that there appears to be a gap between, on the one hand, general knowledge of effective methods of technology transfer (which are known to most agents in general terms) and, on the other hand, putting this knowledge into daily practice.

To address this gap, two direct interventions are immediately possible and appropriate. For one, the complexity of the number of issues involved in successful technology transfer can be reduced if these are presented and organized in a systematic and didactic form. This was done in the list of twenty-three factors described in Chapter 2 and in the Appendix.

1. A large number of Ghanaian and international experts was consulted, including Mr Dan Baffour-Awuah, Mrs Akua Peprah Dua-Agyeman, Mrs Sabina Anokye-Mensah, Mr Kwasi Poku, Mrs Esther Adjeti, Mrs Diana Tempelman, Mrs Lydia Sasu, Mrs Frances Minnow-Hagan, Mrs Yvonne Wallace Bruce, Mrs Sarah Ampha Nunoo, Mrs Teresa Eno Asah, Mrs Magdalena Abrokwa, Mrs Janet Mohammed, Mr Peter Reiling. They are once again thanked for their valuable contributions.

Second, a training programme needs to be built around this checklist, since a list by itself will have little effect on practice. As well as putting across information, the training programme must stimulate the participants to form a habit of translating the general guidelines into the practice of their own daily work. The training should hold a strong appeal for the participants, for instance by using a participatory approach and by offering follow-up activities. It must also build links between the participants, so that they are able to continue to stimulate each other to put what is learned into practice, even after the training is over. In such a way, training could make a contribution to the necessary improvements of practice.

TOOLConsult has undertaken to develop such a training programme. A four-day training course was designed for the Ghanaian context and was tested in 1995 and 1996 in co-operation with local NGOs: in particular TechnoServe Ghana, but also SNV-Ghana, and the FAO regional office.[2] After testing, the manual was fine-tuned, resulting in a trainer's manual called *Introducing Technology to Women's Enterprises*, dated June 1997. TechnoServe Ghana was asked to continue administering this training in Ghana to new groups of development staff. Recently, TOOLConsult has taken initiatives to adapt the training for use in other countries.

Objective and target group The objective of the training is 'to increase the effectiveness of intermediate organizations in their attempts to strengthen women's enterprises through interventions that include the introduction of improved technologies'.

The training is developed for local development staff who work directly with women, women's groups or with women's business associations, and who are interested in stimulating women's enterprises with measures that include improved technology. The staff

---

2. The first try-out was carried out in November 1995 by TOOLConsult's gender consultant Saskia Everts, with assistance from SNV staff member Marion Veltenaar, who was based at the regional branch of the Department of the NCWD (National Council on Women and Development) in Ho. The second try-out, also in November 1995, took place in Accra and was carried out by Saskia Everts in co-operation with trainer Ekua Prah from TechnoServe. The third try-out was carried out in Sunyani by two trainers from TechnoServe: Esther Adjeti (principal trainer) and Wusa Manga (supporting trainer), while FAO Regional Officer Diana Tempelman observed and reported on the training in order to give additional feedback on the course material.

members who participate in training can come from different intermediary organizations, or all from one organization. These organizations can be non-governmental (NGOs) or governmental; preferably the participants come from both kinds of organizations. One of the aims of the training is to bring together development workers from different organizations working in the same general area within one country. Such development workers often do not have a tradition of co-operating, or sharing their knowledge and experiences with each other. Sometimes they are not even aware that others are doing work similar to their own in the same region. During the training they will start to share their immediate experiences, get to know each other better and perhaps establish networks that will continue later on.

In the test phase, the training was tried in two provincial capitals, Ho and Sunyani, and in the national capital, Accra. Although it was found that the training could be adapted on the spot to the different levels of these different groups, it was most appropriate to the groups in the provincial capitals. Here it most clearly fulfilled a need by providing much-needed information, exercises, and an opportunity for exchange of experiences.

In Sunyani, three-quarters of the participants (representing governmental and non-governmental organizations as well as farmers' groups) were illiterate. This try-out showed that, with some adaptations, the training also has strong potential for illiterate target groups (Tempelman 1996).

Contents of the training

Overview of the training programme The day-to-day training programme is given in the box opposite. Explanations and illustrations of some of the sessions follow.

Twenty-three factors The training opens and closes with the 'twenty-three factors for the introduction of technology to women's enterprises'. These factors, which are also described in Chapter 2 and listed and illustrated in the Appendix, cover the things that have to be in place for a technology transfer project to be successful. They range from 'market situation' to 'socio-cultural conditions'. In principle, this list of factors can be used as a reference or checklist by

The training programme

Day 1

Morning

Session 1: Getting acquainted

Session 2: Participants' own problem definitions: nothing is easy about the introduction of technology to women's enterprises

Session 3: Twenty-three factors for the introduction of technology to women's enterprises

Afternoon

Session 4: Women, gender and technology

Day 2

Morning

Session 5: Market research

Afternoon

Session 6: Rapid Market Appraisal: information-gathering in town

Day 3

Morning

Session 7: Calculating the finances of technical investments

Afternoon

Session 8: The technical issues: technology choice and bridging the gender gap

Day 4

Morning

Session 9: The 'twenty-three factors for the introduction of technology to women's enterprises' in your own practice

Afternoon

Session 10: Personal action plans, collective follow-up, and closing the training development staff when undertaking technology introduction. However, to increase the chances of this list – or some other list covering the same range of factors – actually becoming internalized and thus influencing practice, the trainees are first asked to make their own list, based on their own experience. An excerpt from the trainer's manual illustrates this:

> In this section, you will work from the experience of the participants themselves etc. Remember: they are already experts on the practice of technology transfer! At the end of the section, participants will be given the syllabus, in which twenty-three factors are listed and described, and illustrated with examples. However, this list is only *one* possible way of organizing the factors involved in technology transfer. One could just as well make up a somewhat different list, as long as all the factors are in there and as long as the list helps the participants to remember and include all of them. The best way for participants to remember them all is, in fact, if they themselves have gone through the struggle of trying to list them all in an organized way. Therefore, before the list in the syllabus is presented, ask the participants to make their own lists, using the following instructions:
>
> Let the participants work in small groups. Ask each group the following: 'List all the reasons why a project for introducing technology to women can fail.' Explain that each reason for failure corresponds to a factor for success that needs to be in place for a technology transfer project to be successful: a factor that either has to be in place or has to be put in place. […] Ask them to make their pile of factors as complete as possible.

Because the training for practitioners should not take up too much time at one stretch, the content to be covered needs to be limited. Thus, rather than addressing all twenty-three factors superficially, the training treats a few of the factors in the necessary depth. Central themes of the training are, first of all, gender issues, and second the need to take a business approach when one wants to introduce improved technologies to women. Also, attention is paid to the technical factors (category D in the list of factors, see Appendix). Two additional four-day training sessions would probably be sufficient to cover all the factors of successful technology introduction.

Gender issues In the list of twenty-three factors, gender is not presented as *one* of the factors; rather, the gender aspects of each factor are discussed where relevant. In the training, gender aspects are both dealt with separately and integrated in the other themes. Specific sessions on gender take place on the afternoon of the first day. These include an exercise on 'spotting gender'. The objective of this exercise is to teach people to recognize where and how gender is at work around them. That is, they learn how societies differentiate between men and women, and how this differentiation influences the way people behave and feel, how it influences their opportunities and access to resources, and how it influences the way development programmes work out for men and women. An important lesson is learned when participants see how gender structures their own behaviour and options. Gender issues are also addressed in session 7 on calculating finances, and in the technology sessions.

Rapid Market Appraisal (RMA) The Rapid Market Appraisal methodology developed by TOOLConsult enables entrepreneurs, including micro-scale or illiterate entrepreneurs, to do their own basic market research. Thus they can find out whether there is a market for a new, improved or altered product. Skills in market appraisal are an important part of any small-scale enterprise support; and when development workers consider introducing new technologies to a very small business, the market question is crucial. Almost all technical investments in women's micro-enterprises are economically viable only if production is increased, and – this is too often forgotten – if this increased production can also be sold. Absence of a market for increased production is probably one of the most common reasons for failure of the introduction of new technologies. Likewise, new technologies may improve the quality of a product, but if this also requires a (slight) price increase, it is not automatically true that female entrepreneurs can access a market for this product. What looks like improved quality from a technical point of view does not necessarily result in a more marketable product. Rapid Market Appraisal can give the business woman or the development worker an idea of whether there is a market for a product changed in quality or quantity.

The training on introducing technology to women's enterprises spends the whole of the second day on the theory and, especially, the practice of the RMA instrument. The importance of the market is emphasized, and it is stressed that there is only one way to discover if your changed product will sell and at what price: ask the potential customers. Participants are shown a systematic way to get the information they need.

Technology sessions The third training day includes a number of exercises that focus on technology. Some of these challenge the participants to become critical and independently thinking technology consumers. Both project staff and the women they work with are urged to take an active stand *vis-à-vis* the technology that they are confronted with. This does not mean that they need to understand the technical details, nor even necessarily that they should always be able to run the machines themselves. It is more important that they are able to ask those who provide the technologies the right questions, that they are able to choose between available options, and that, if need be, they are able to refuse a technical 'improvement' because it may not be an improvement to them. Exercises, role play and structured information exchange form the elements of these sessions.

Another of the technology sessions of this module focuses on bridging the psychological gap between women and technology. Many women think that they are not technical. They sometimes find machines dangerous or are afraid they might damage them, and their reaction to technology is often, 'It's not for me'. While women may participate in a technical training and learn the appropriate technical behaviour, they often still experience technology as something alien to them and discard it as soon as the trainer disappears. In the training on introducing technologies to women's enterprises, a simple but effective electricity exercise is used to illustrate some of the things involved in bridging the psychological gender gap.

At the start of the electricity exercise the participants are told that they are going to make a 'light burn by connecting the electricity to it'. It is stressed that, at this moment, probably almost no one in the group knows how to do this. Yet, in less than twenty minutes, everyone will know and this will be achieved almost without explanations or help from others. The real lesson is to reflect on what happens during those twenty minutes in their heads, their minds and their hearts. Some time is spent explaining this 'rare human quality of reflection'.

The participants are divided into small groups, and a set of batteries, wires, lamps, switches and tools (some of them not used in this task!) are put on a table. A very basic drawing is presented, showing only the elementary idea that electricity has to flow through a circuit. One of the most interesting things that the participants gain from this exercise is an enormous sense of achievement when they solve the problem themselves.

In one of the courses there was a very telling difference between two groups: in the first group, one man knew beforehand how to do the exercise, while in the second group, composed entirely of women, no one knew. In the first group, the experienced man quickly took possession of the tools and connected the wire as it should be done. The light burned and that was that. Shortly afterwards, a great cheer sounded from the other side of the room. The group in which no one knew what to do beforehand had, after a lot of stumbling, laughing, despairing and reasoning, discovered how to make the light burn. They felt a great pride and sense of achievement. The members of this group will surely never lose the feeling of having been able to deal with a technical problem. They had, in a sense, bridged a gap between themselves and the little electric light. On the other hand, those from the first group may have learned something by looking on while an experienced man did the work, but they had missed the psychological experience of discovering something for themselves. Their new knowledge was shallow and boring and a feeling of distance towards the technology remained.

The electricity exercise gives the participants important insights into learning as well as teaching technology – and in the gender aspects of this. Was it a coincidence that the joyful and egalitarian discovery took place in an all-women's group, while the women in the group where an experienced man was present had quite a different learning experience?

Methods and approach of the training

One of the most important but difficult-to-achieve objectives of training programmes is to ensure that participants change their actions in the future. This is certainly also one of the objectives of the training on introducing technologies to women's enterprises. As was described earlier, the problem with most technical projects for women is not so much that the development workers do not know why they fail, but that they apply insufficient time and effort to avoiding the reasons for failure. Therefore, a specific effort is made to influence future practice as much as possible, although necessarily within the limits that any training has in this regard.

Inducing the attitude that improvement is needed Although attitudes are difficult to change, it is important to make an attempt in that direction, since the *desire* to be effective will be helpful in achieving a behavioural change.

To achieve this, the following methods are included in the training:

- starting with the problems that participants themselves actually perceive
- strongly addressing the effects of ineffective introduction of technology to women's enterprises
- learning as personal discovery through step-by-step build-up of training sessions
- exercises that promote identification with project target groups

In the try-outs, most of the exercises that followed this line were quite successful. For example, in the session on participants' own problem definitions, many people mentioned the problem that 'groups are not co-operating' and that there is 'bad time management among women's groups'. Some way into the training, the group came to realize that some of the problems with groups not co-operating may have to do with the wrong choice of project rather than with the untrustworthiness of the groups. Better project identification and feasibility studies could in many cases have avoided this. In this way, the need for project preparation becomes linked to a problem, and this increases people's willingness to do something about it.

Here is another example that shows learning through personal discovery and identifying with project target groups. In Accra it was discussed whether development staff should start with group enterprises among women or with individual enterprises. The issue was dealt with as follows. The participants were asked to list all the advantages of group enterprises, and then they were asked to think for a minute about the following: 'Imagine that you are given the opportunity to start a business. You are asked to invest in this business 80 per cent of all the money you have saved up to now (you yourself will know how much that is). On top of that, you are offered a loan, equalling that first amount, to invest that into the business as well. Now, think about this: if you decide to enter this business, who would you like to join up with (supposing that those you join with also invest 80 per cent of their money, etc.)? How many people would you preferably go together with? One, two, ten? Or would you 'go it alone'?'

This was a great eye-opener to many participants. In spite of all the advantages of group enterprises that they had just listed, almost all of them said that, given the choice, they would start an enterprise either alone or with one, or at the most two, people. Putting themselves in the place of the project target group clearly brought home to them the disadvantages of group enterprises and the need to find alternative ways of organizing production. 'I have never looked at it this way,' one of the participants exclaimed.

Experiencing the new approaches When a trainer advises participants of the best way to undertake certain aspects of their work, the participants will usually agree, but this does not mean that they will actually do things this way. Trainees must at least experience the suggested ways of working. This will make application after the training easier and more likely. To promote the experience of new approaches, the following methods are used:

- stimulating a high level of participation during all training sessions, whether plenary, through group work, in role plays or individually
- using exercises
- applying the subjects discussed to one's own practice
- using cases from participants' experience
- making personal work plans
- including field work and practical applications

In all three try-outs, the participants were actively involved and enjoyed the exercises and field work. The use of personal real-life cases was also successful; in Ho, for example, participants managed to put together an impressive list of cases illustrating each of the twenty-three factors. Some of these cases are added to the list as presented in the Appendix.

For the Accra group, the section on making personal work plans based on what was learned in the training was very successful, with participants planning improvements such as: '[this training] will make me review and revise some proposals I am about to send out for funding. The very approach to existing projects where we have involvement may also need looking at. Our next project to be embarked on will find me actively involved in the market research aspect instead of being a mere passenger on the train to give me more experience.'

Another example of this is letting the participants experience new methods of teaching technology to women through the exercise on making electrical circuits, described above.

Peer group influence In order to achieve changes in behaviour, instilling knowledge and new attitudes is not enough. Direct influences on behaviour are a forceful factor as well. One of these is peer group influence. The training attempts to channel peer group influence by the following methods:

- selecting participants who all work in one area
- setting a joint atmosphere of serious and enthusiastic mutual work
- sharing successes and failures
- stimulating communal follow-up activities

For example, on the final day of the training, participants each present one real-life problem. An effort is made by the trainer to create an atmosphere in which these problems can be discussed openly and constructively, in order to generate inspiring suggestions on how to deal with them. This activity will not only present the participants with possible solutions to some of their problems, it will also show how helpful it can be to exchange experiences with colleagues working for different organizations. Ideally, this exercise will lead to a proposal to continue such exchanges. The trainer creates room for this suggestion to arise, but it must come from the group itself.

A sense of mutuality and group feeling was certainly achieved during the try-out in Ho. Indicative of this was the spontaneous closing ceremony. The trainers surprised the participants with a special cake with the inscription 'Gender and Technology, Ho 1995', the participants started to dance and sing spontaneously and finally gave a present to the trainers. Most importantly, a plan was launched to continue this mutual learning process, and to support each other in applying the new concepts learned.

The follow-up

Another important but difficult aim of the training is to establish some kind of follow-up. The last day in particular leads up to this through the following training sessions:

• discussing real-life problems
• making private action plans
• deciding on communal follow-up

Objectives of the follow-up include: enabling the participants to digest all the new information given so far; helping them put it into practice, and if possible helping them develop a habit of adopting more thorough appraisal and implementation strategies.

In Ho, this need was also articulated by the participants themselves who, half-way through the training, had already started to discuss the fact that they wanted this learning process to continue. The participants not only liked the training, but also liked each other and the way they were working together. During the last sections on 'private action plans' and 'communal follow-up', this desire was voiced again and the participants decided to form a 'network', with the aim of exchanging experiences and supporting each other in their work. Two of the participants were asked to organize the first meeting of the network.

Network-forming is facilitated as an outcome of the training. Such a network does not, in the longer run, need to include all participants. It may rather consist of only a few members who get along well and who are dedicated to improving their effectiveness in technology transfer. It should preferably remain informal and should not seek financial support but keep its costs very low.

To achieve this, throughout the training sections the following question is stressed: 'How do we help ourselves and each other to use this knowledge, insights and skills after the training?' Finally, co-operation is required from an organization in that locality willing to take the lead in a follow-up. An excerpt from the trainer's manual illustrates this:

A training, however successful, is always no more than a moment in time. Before long, your participants will be drawn back into their daily busy work life. Because of the circumstances that they work in, they will tend to go back to their practices as they were before. How much of what they have learned so far will they actually apply? The chance that the training has some actual influence will be much greater, if the participants would in future continue to support and remind each other of the things learned. If only a few of them would keep meeting each other in future, for example once every two months, and discuss their work, openly address the problems they encounter, and inspire each other to increase the quality of their work, this training will have been successful. This is why this training is best given for a group of participants who all work and live in one region.

Conclusions

The results of the three try-outs of this training programme are promising. According to the evaluation forms as well as personal communications, participants were at the very least satisfied and most were enthusiastic. Other indications of the appropriateness of the training are the continued attendance and the level of participation of the trainees. Noteworthy is the fact that, for example, Rapid Market Appraisal was quite well understood and carried out also by illiterate participants. While the section on business calculations had to be much simplified for this group, the main objective of this section – to show the importance of doing calculations before deciding on the introduction of technology – clearly came across. The group in Ho, which although literate was mostly not highly educated, was able to grasp the idea of the calculations to a relatively high degree. All in all, the try-outs suggest that with a step-by-step approach even complicated subjects can be grasped by groups that previously have had little experience of them.

However, the real measure of the success of any training is whether or not it actually improves practice. This is also the most difficult result to measure, and for the present training there has been no opportunity to do so. It is clear, however, that it is not easy to achieve follow-up activity intended to strengthen the effects of the training. In the Sunyani try-out, such a follow-up was not really tried because too many participants came from far away. In Accra, the commitment of the participants was not great enough to compete with other demands on their time. In Ho there was much commitment and enthusiasm, but even there the next concrete action (another meeting to exchange work experiences and to discuss ways to make technology transfer more effective) took place only when triggered by a visit from the international trainer.

This shows the need for training like this to become firmly embedded in a local organization committed to promoting the training's ideas. Such an organization can take the lead in setting up follow-up meetings, it can give the same training again for new development staff, and it can set up follow-up courses for those who have already participated.

Another important finding is that when the training has been given once by an experienced trainer, the detailed trainer's manual gives sufficient information and advice to enable new trainers to give the training independently, and also to adapt it to new circumstances without losing the general line and idea behind it.

4. Involving women in the market-driven promotion of improved technology

Market forces as ally

In Chapters 1 and 2 it was concluded that the development of new technical variations of 'appropriate' tools appears to be more successful than securing a widespread use of such tools. There is a gap between the innovative capacity of development organizations and their capacity to disseminate the innovations. Overall, the potential advantages of improved technologies are reaching women 'too late, too little'.

This is partly due to the limited successes of many of the dissemination projects that do exist, which often do not adequately take into account all the factors that are a precondition for adoption of technology (see Chapter 2). But there is also a broader issue at stake. However successful dissemination projects might at some stage become, their scope will most probably always be limited. Dissemination through development organizations requires intensive inputs from development organizations, donors and/or governments for indefinite periods of time. Since the inputs of some of these actors are unstable, the sustainability of such an approach will normally be low. Also, development organizations are not always in the best position to achieve technology development and dissemination. And even when they are, the intricacies of technology dissemination make effective projects extremely demanding of the scarce resources of development organizations such as time, skills and funds. Therefore, the scale on which effects can be generated through development organizations –

whether they are international organizations and bilateral donors, national governments, or NGOs; and whether they have ineffective or excellent practices – necessarily remains limited.

What is required in order to achieve more widespread and sustainable effects is the emergence of a *dynamic of dissemination* that takes over the effort of development organizations. In particular, the dynamics of the 'market' could form a system of independent dynamics that might achieve this. Development organizations can seldom be so broadly effective and cheap as decentralized mechanisms that involve the capacities of hundreds of individual entrepreneurs and customers. The challenge is to make market forces take over, in a sustainable manner, some of the work which is now being done by small groups of trained development workers. In this line of thought, market forces are seen as a potentially useful ally, which can be complementary to more conventional strategies for technology development. The ally may not have the exact same programme, but it may be going in the same direction. The idea is that if we were to hop on to the train of the market, and maybe slightly redirect some of the actors, and if necessary jump off in time, we would arrive much faster at where we want to be.

From 1994 to 1998 the ILO and TOOLConsult together carried out a programme called FIT (Farm Implements and Tools) which promotes improved farming and food-processing technologies. FIT has been experimenting with approaches that make use of and promote market dynamics that effectively support the development and dissemination of improved tools. Although the results of the FIT programme are not conclusive, it has generated a few ideas and examples which illustrate the potential of the market-driven approach. They also give an opportunity to make a preliminary inquiry into the possibilities and pitfalls of this approach for women.

Gender While the market-driven approach for promoting improved tools is being further developed and gaining in popularity, it should be considered from the beginning how such an approach will work out for women. How do gender relations play into market forces and how might gender relations be influenced by programmes that intend to catalyse and use market forces? And, importantly, how can market-driven approaches be used to *strengthen* women and make gender relations more egalitarian?

This chapter discusses two examples of market-driven activities and their possibilities for helping women, in particular food processors. The first is to approach women as customers rather than beneficiaries, bringing them into direct contact with commercial providers of tools. The second is to make use of the resources of larger companies. Even though these are relatively newly developed initiatives – or rather, *because* they are new and still in the process of being developed – this is the moment to start thinking of the gender issues involved.

Seeing beneficiaries as customers: 'user-led innovation meetings'

In 1994, FIT arranged a meeting in Embu, Kenya, between ten metal workers who specialize in the production of farming tools and a group of farmers. Five of the sixteen farmers were women. In a lively discussion, the two groups discussed the advantages and disadvantages of new types of agricultural equipment that the farmers had tried out. Improvements in the designs were suggested. The metal workers afterwards described the day as an 'eye-opener' which enabled them to learn much about what the farmers would like to buy from them; they observed that they had not taken the problems of farmers seriously before. After receiving some help in acquiring the raw materials for prototypes, the metal workers started to sketch out some designs which they felt had potential. Ten new or adapted pieces of equipment were developed.

One month later, an open day was organized in which the metal workers showed and demonstrated the new models to farmers. A panel of eight farmers, four men and four women, judged the tools. Taking their task very seriously, they carefully awarded scores to each prototype, clearly defining the advantages and disadvantages of each. For example, the winning tool was the Mutomo Mk II plough, a plough with wooden beam based on the Mutomo Mk I, but with a mouldboard blade instead of a ridger. The conclusions of the panel were: 'Light to use, can be used by women and older people. Penetration is very good. Looks easy to repair. Can be used for wet and dry ploughing and for weeding. Mouldboard attachment should be altered, to make it inter-changeable with manufactured ones.' On the other hand, the Rocky Plough, also based on the Mutomo Mk I and with a mouldboard, but made from heavy metal and with a big iron tube, was judged as follows: 'Too heavy; needs a strong animal to work it. Animals need to be trained to use this plough.' The metal workers continued to work on the tools and some sales were made in the months following the meetings (Tanburn and van Bussel 1995).

Customers buy products and by that token have a certain amount of power *vis-à-vis* those who want to sell their products. The rejection of a product by the customer means lack of sales and income for the provider. Therefore, enterprises that are dependent on the market have a strong incentive to provide well for the needs and wishes of technology users. In a way (and paradoxically), the incentive to cater to such needs is actually stronger than it is for an 'aid' organization. This is one important reason to make use of market-driven tool makers, such as the informal sector metal workers.

In practice, however, there is often little communication between local tool providers and their customers about the needs and wishes of those customers. To promote this contact and the user-led innovation that can arise from it, FIT has been organizing meetings between small entrepreneurs in the agro-metal sector and farmers in Kenya, also called 'Participatory Technology Development' meetings. As the story above indicates, the first results are promising.

From a gender perspective, however, there are some extra questions we need to ask. The market forces approach is not gender-neutral; it is not obvious that women can benefit as much from this approach as men can. Women users of food-processing devices and farming equipment are in a different position from men, and therefore the workings of the market will be somewhat different for them. This should be a matter of concern to development workers. If women benefit less than men, this new approach will prolong the uneven distribution of the benefits of development between men and women. While, for instance, male farmers will see their tools improve, women farmers may not, which leads to a (relative) deterioration of the position of women. Development workers are responsible for at least trying to avoid such an effect. And they may also feel obliged to contribute to a *strengthening* of the position of women. In either case, attempts to approach beneficiaries as customers must from the outset consider gender aspects.

There are at least two factors that are influenced by gender and that may limit the positive effects of user-led innovation for women.

The first is the question of the access of women to user-led innovation meetings, such as the meeting described in the example above. The second point is women's '*consumer power*'.

Access of women to meetings for user-led innovation In 1995, FIT arranged a meeting in Kisumu, Kenya, between a group of metal workers with a particular interest in the development of farm implements and tools, and a group of twenty-two farmers. Although many women farmers were specifically invited, in many cases the husbands came instead. Only five of the farmers who arrived were women. Clearly, the husbands of the invited women wanted to be involved in this officially arranged and possibly lucrative activity.

Following this meeting, the metal workers were again keen to design and build equipment which corresponded to the needs expressed by the farmers. Two were so inspired by what they had heard, that they started to build prototypes without any external financial assistance. Thus, as intended, the metal workers were preparing to cater to the needs of the farmers. However, it is questionable whether the needs of women farmers were adequately represented (Tanburn 1995).

User-led innovation meetings should be carefully designed so as to involve women users of equipment. It is clear from the case described above that simply explicitly inviting women may often not be enough. There are a few additional options that could be tried and are being tried now. More experiments and experiences are needed to find the best methods for a particular context.

First of all, the design of a user-led innovation meeting should take into account all the general provisions that are necessary to enable women to participate in any meeting. Gender-sensitive thinking should go into the choice of time, place and occasion of the meeting, as well as into all other characteristics of the meeting, such as costs involved for the participants, its provisions for children, and the way of announcing the meeting.

Gender-sensitive thinking means that the social differences between men and women, their roles, needs and possibilities, are taken into account when planning an intervention. Gender-sensitive thinking alerts planners to the gender-specific roles of both men and women: while men are expected to do male tasks, and have male rights and duties, women have quite another set of (often more heavy) duties

and (almost always fewer) rights. Given that women have both productive and reproductive duties, meetings that are to be attended by
women should not be too long, not too far from the home, and not
at hours when women have other duties such as cooking meals or
working in the fields. Because women in many countries are not free
to travel at all hours, or not to all places, this should also be taken
into account. For example, in most situations women must be able to
get back before dark. Women's access to money for bus or taxi fares
may also be more limited than that of men.

In some countries, a good occasion for a meeting that intends to
attract women farmers is near the market at the end of a market day
(to reach women farmers who sell their own produce) or just after
the start of the market (to reach women farmers who have sold
produce at wholesale to retailers).

If the meetings are made into a women's affair from the beginning,
women are more likely to participate. It will therefore be useful to
centralize the meetings round equipment which is known to be of
concern to women. The invitations could be done by women, come
from a women's organization or use female channels such as traditional women's savings or social groups. Also, at the meetings, any
demonstrations of tools should preferably be done by women. This
again reinforces the idea that women are the experts and that it is
their concern.

Nevertheless, in situations where men are the ones who usually
buy the tools that women use, or where men prefer to be in control
of their wives' dealings, it may be better explicitly to invite women
and their husbands. This way the men will know what the meeting is
about and not worry too much if the wives go alone the next time.
In most cases, there should be a second women-only meeting. This is
because women may tend to keep silent when the men are present,
and the information they do give may be less complete. That means
that at least two user-led innovation meetings must be planned.

Women's 'consumer power' Women's consumer power is
related to gender patterns. Women themselves are, on the whole,
poorer than men; therefore their 'buying power' is usually less. When
the income of women is low, it may at first sight seem economically
less interesting for producers to cater to the needs of this group.
This does not need to be the case, however. When a new tool is

economically viable, it is a realistic option even for the very poor, if they can access micro-credit. Fortunately, women have proved to be credit-worthy, also in banking systems that do not demand collateral. To ensure that market-driven technology improvements also benefit women, intermediary organizations should take care to link women to credit facilities.

More importantly even, women's consumer power will be influenced by their access to and control over income within the household. This degree of control differs, depending on the prevailing gender patterns. In some ethnic or socio-economic groups, for example, men will buy the tools that women will use; whether women will in that case be the ones to make the final purchasing decision is questionable. On the other hand, even if the husband controls the money, the wife may still exercise a substantial influence on the decision. In other cases, the resources of a man and a woman in a single household are strictly separated, and the woman will make the purchasing decisions that relate to her own tasks, using her own income for the investment. These various scenarios lead to great differences in the way user-led innovation works out for women. Thus, a basic knowledge of *intra-household dynamics* is indispensable when trying to promote user-led technical innovation in a gender-sensitive way. In many cases some research will need to be done. This kind of research benefits more from a few in-depth interviews than from a greater number of superficial questionnaires. The interviews should be conducted by women who should talk to the women farmers separately from the men, with no family members or neighbours within hearing distance. The research should look at who controls, decides and pays what, and try to find out about the actual situation on these points as well as about the gender *ideology*. Ideology and practice together make up the picture of intra-household dynamics.

The purpose of such research is to find the *niches of financial autonomy* that women possess. For example, through traditional credit and saving circles, as well as through new credit schemes specifically for women (in groups), many women can establish a financial resource which they can control and which remains separate from the resources that are considered family property. Such niches should form the entrance points for mobilizing women's consumer power.

While all alternative schemes proposed by development programmes should be economically sustainable, alternatives that depend on market dynamics are automatically forced in that direction. When the customer, through her purchasing behaviour, determines whether or not a certain technical adaptation is going to be widely applied, any such adaptation must have a positive cost–benefit balance. If the envisioned (female) users have very little buying power, user-led innovations will only work for equipment that leads to *financial* gains. This can be the case for tools that support commercial production, such as micro-enterprises in food processing. It is also the case that tools for non-commercial household activities can lead to financial gains, as long as the tools are either cost-saving or labour-saving, while opportunities exist to use the saved labour in financially reward-ing alternative activities. A customer with almost no leeway in her finances must herself be able to translate the supposed advantages of a tool into financial terms. She must, for example, have a general idea of the payback time of the investment. When the tool is to be used in a small commercial enterprise, the payback times are usually based on a projected production volume; for example, the volume produced when the new equipment runs full-time and at full speed. The entrepreneur herself should be able to judge whether she is likely to have sufficient time and access to raw materials to achieve such a production volume, and, most importantly, if she can market such a volume. If not, the payback time of the investment can turn out to be much longer.

Next to income level, access to credit and control over finances, *information* determines the degree of a consumer's power. If the quality of the products is to be improved, the buyer must be critical, must know what to be critical about and must know how to judge the essential features of a tool. Women generally have less access to written information, but word-of-mouth can be a good medium. Therefore, and not only for efficiency reasons, the user-led innovation meetings should bring together *groups* of customers with producers. It may even be worthwhile first to bring these female buyer groups together without (male) producers being present, so that the women can compare their experiences and strengthen their views.

This leads to the fourth factor in consumer power: the *attitude*. In countries in the South as well as in the North, technology is usually regarded as a carrier of status, progress and improvement. Those who do not readily accept technical novelties are often seen as conservative, uninformed and generally backward. Yet in specific circumstances a new technology may not be an improvement at all. In a generally technophile world, it requires a quite independently critical attitude, as well as a degree of strength and self-confidence, to question to desirability of an 'improved' technology when commercial producers or even development organizations enthusiastically recommend it.

Such an attitude can be strengthened by training. The example in the box describes a training session that addresses women's attitudes towards the 'improved' technologies that may be offered to them. The session is part of the training described in Chapter 3.

Training session on being a critical consumer

In a four-day training programme for intermediary organizations on technology transfer for women's enterprises tried out in Ghana, one half-day was spent on women as critical technology-buyers. The participants, mostly women, were asked to take one tool that they liked and one that they disliked, and to list for themselves all the reasons for their like and dislike. They then took part in a role play in which a 'seller' was trying to convince a 'buyer' of the advantages of the tool, while the buyer was asking critical questions. The buyers were very critical indeed and did not let themselves be convinced into buying something they felt they did not need.

It was then discussed with the participants (who were all NGO and GO development workers involved in introducing technology to women's groups) what they would think if 'their' rural women reacted in the same way to them when they came to promote their improved technologies. Would it not be the greatest development achievement if these women said: 'Well, thank you for your suggestion, project officer, but I don't need this tool, as I have calculated the payback time of investment, taking into account the need for repairs as well as the limited possibilities to increase my sales and production, and concluded that the investment is just not justified.' The trainers asked the participants: 'Would you as a development worker have a success story on your hands, or would you have a failed project?' Understandably, this provoked a lot of discussion.

Thus, only if the access of women to user-led innovation meetings and their consumer power are optimized, are they likely to benefit from market-driven dissemination of improved technology.

Tapping the industry channel: making use of the resources of larger companies

Food processors in Kenya, that is some 50,000 female entrepreneurs in tiny food-processing businesses (Gemini 1994), are at present barely reached by NGO or government programmes. While the government of Kenya has programmes supporting the informal sector, food processing has been more or less excluded, apparently among other reasons because of a notion that food processing is not actually a productive activity. This has given rise to a vicious circle: both as a consequence and a result of the limited attention paid to food processors, they are barely organized and therefore quite difficult even to find or address. FIT has explored the opportunity of using a quite different channel, namely larger industries, to reach and help food processors. Eight multinational, large or medium enterprises were interviewed. The scope for co-operation was explored and some preliminary ideas for mutual activities were outlined.

Coca-Cola Kenya presently provides a training programme for its outlets, which include both stores and (very small) restaurants. The latter programme, which reaches women food processors, has up to now been based only in Nairobi. It consists of a two-hour film, made by Coca Cola-USA, on marketing and customer service ('How to get the customer into my restaurant, how to make the customer buy the product on which I have the most added value, and how to make the restaurant an experience for the customer'). Coca-Cola wants to take this training activity out of Nairobi, and possibly into the rural areas. Probably both form and content of the training activity need to be adjusted for application in rural areas. Coca-Cola does not yet have much experience with this in Kenya, or in other African countries. This is where a development programme, such as FIT, could come in.

Coca-Cola can imagine working together with an NGO on determining content and form of the training. This would give the NGO the opportunity to include wider development goals in the training, such as hygiene, business expansion, marketing, and innovations in food processing, including information on improved food-processing tools. The NGO could also help to evaluate and record this activity, to make it more replicable. Coca-Cola, in return, could provide part of the finances and infrastructure (Everts 1995).

Opportunities offered by the industry channel Larger companies may provide a good channel through which to reach large groups of women for several reasons. For one, many companies are already reaching down to people in a number of ways, with means and resources that are usually quite substantial compared to those of governments and NGOs.

East African Industries (EAI) has an intensive programme of marketing activities with which it reaches large numbers of women. EAI approaches all women's groups that are registered by the government to demonstrate its products. It also gives demonstrations at the markets at the end of the market day. Four demonstrators in Kenya talk to three groups a day on four days a week. Since a group may consist of 50 to 200 women, the number reached should be no less than 600 a week. These are numbers that most NGOs can only dream of. Next to information about EAI's products (which include food products such as margarine and soup-flavouring cubes), EAI supplies information on nutrition, showing the five types of food needed, and so on. It also hands out samples and presents (Everts 1995).

Furthermore, if an intervention could be grafted on to the interests of industry, in a way that also benefits the industrial partner, then it is more likely to be sustainable than an activity that is dependent on funding from charities or governments.

Another interesting point is the healthy mixture of cultures that could arise from co-operation with industry. The businesslike, cost-conscious and efficient culture that many industries have been forced to develop in order to survive the everyday reality of economic life might be a very good addition to the more welfare- and funding-oriented cultures of some NGOs. At the same time, if the more social and responsible orientation of development NGOs could find a route into and a place within this industrial culture, a more balanced mix might arise there as well.

Why would larger companies be interested in such co-operation? The reasons that the industries interviewed in Nairobi gave for their interest in co-operating with development initiatives (in this case initiatives to support food processors), include the following:

- 'If their business grows, our business grows.' Many larger businesses are linked to small businesses, for example if food processors use the larger company's product in their business. In these cases improvements in food processors' businesses may also mean better sales for the larger company. Although most food processors have little consuming power, there are larger firms that do cater to this bottom-end of the market. If the numbers are great enough, the group may be very important to a large company. For example, flour producer UNGA's most important flour product, EXE, is for the greatest part used for chapatis and mandazis, which are prepared for sale by the minuscule businesses of food processors.
- Corporate image. Some of the larger Kenyan businesses and multinationals are aware of the importance of how people perceive the company; whether it is sympathetic to them or not. The famous example of the Kenyan Tobacco Company, which organizes a large yearly show to promote the *jua kali* (informal sector), is well known and seen as a successful activity.
- Government relations. It can improve relations with the government if the company shows that it supports government goals, such as, in Kenya, reinforcing the informal sector.
- A desire to contribute to the development of Kenya, or to give something back to the country that has enabled a company to grow: 'We have to give the people of Kenya something back.'
- Negligible investments. Some of the ideas may require only limited extra investments which, compared to the budgets and profits of some large companies, are negligible.
- Need to spend social budgets. Some companies have special budgets which have to be spent on 'socially oriented' activities. For example, Coca-Cola is to spend 3 per cent of its profits worldwide on education and health-related activities; those must not be linked to the requirement to buy or sell Coca-Cola.

The challenge in tapping the industry channel, then, is to find where the interests of, on the one hand, development organizations and, on the other hand, industry (or other large companies) overlap. Development workers must seek constructions which are linked to some interest of industry, and that do not require excessive *extra* investments. The first experiences in Kenya suggest that this may be quite possible. Of the eight multinational, large- or medium-scale enterprises that were contacted on this consultancy, all were interested in co-operation, only one was doubtful about possibilities, and most were positive.

Risks in working with larger companies Any intervention can have unintended unfavourable effects. Development interventions that link up with industry, and therefore by definition promote the interests of the industry as well as the interests of the development target group, must assess the possible unfavourable effects of promoting the industry. The clearest case is when an industrial product is in direct competition with the business of the target group that the development organization wants to support.

For example, UNGA is a large maize miller and in that role it is in direct competition with thousands of local 'posho' mills. Using (and thereby promoting) UNGA's maize-related channels for development is therefore not a good option. On the other hand, grain cannot economically be milled on MSE level in Kenya (Kristjanson et al. 1995: appendix 1, p. 6), this product does therefore not pose a direct threat to the poorer Kenyan population.

Another example is the attempt of TOTAL to replace charcoal cooking by gas cooking. In Kenya, some 34,000 women are involved in the charcoal trade, and any increase in TOTAL's market share is most likely to result in a loss in their market. In this case, however, the ecological aspects should also be considered, and the best option might be to look into the possibilities of alternative income-generating activities for this group of women charcoal traders.

The first rule of thumb for working with industry would therefore be to look into the direct competition that such an industry poses to MSEs.

Strengthening women as central actors through contacts between large and small enterprises Is it possible for women to be not only passive recipients of the messages of larger industries – such as is still very much the case in the example of EAI – but to to be strengthened as economic actors? This depends very much on the kind of information transferred. Possibly, also, a more two-way pattern of communication could be achieved, or a form of co-operation or partnership.

There are many ideas for, and also experiences with, forms of co-operation that go beyond a one-way message administered by large industries, and actually have the potential to strengthen the small entrepreneurs or farmers reached. Most experience up to now has been gained in Asia, but indications are that it could certainly be transplanted to Africa.

Nestlé in Sri Lanka has organized the supply of milk from some 12,000 registered farmers in three districts. They have organized themselves into co-operatives which are responsible for the operation of collecting points donated by Nestlé. Nestlé further provides extensive technical and financial assistance to the farmers to ensure the regular supply of quality milk. In exchange for this assistance there is a gentlemen's agreement that the farmers will sell their milk to Nestlé through the collection points.

In Botswana, Barclays Bank initiated a programme to assist SSEs and thereby in the long term to gain additional customers. Local branch managers were induced to overcome their traditional reluctance to make loans to SSEs by the provision of a partial guarantee of such loans from Barclays Development Fund. The managers were able to use their local knowledge to assess the viability of new projects put forward by local entrepreneurs but were also able to be more relaxed in their stringent requirement for collateral with the partial guarantee available from the Development Fund (Voeten 1993: 6, 7).

In Kenya, UNGA told FIT that it would like to undertake a campaign which included an element of SSE support. It could be a competition, consisting of a few questions on an entry form; the winner would win a set of machines and materials with which to start a business. Meanwhile, the campaign might be so set up that it would have some benefit for all entrepreneurs joining in the competition. For example, by adding on to the entry form (or on the packaging material of the flour packs) some message that is of interest to those who run micro-enterprises: it could be a business tip, information on existing small credit programmes, a recipe for fruit-filled mandazis, tips on registration and information on taxation, or it could even be a discount on the popular book *How to Start Your Own Business*. A series of tips, if attractively presented, could be cut out of packages and collected. UNGA was open to such suggestions:

it welcomed the idea of giving something back to the Kenyan people, and felt this would also strengthen UNGA's corporate image (Everts 1995).

It should never be taken for granted that an effective plan will be as effective for women as it is for men. There are many gender-related factors in the success of a plan, leading to differential distribution of positive outcomes. For a specific intervention, these differential outcomes may be predicted, for example by using the TOOLConsult EGA instrument described in the next chapter. A gender analysis of the target group can give an explanation of why an intervention reaches significantly fewer women. It will also give ideas on how a programme could be readjusted to increase the chances of benefiting women.

The first steps to take Although more experience needs to be gained, it is already possible to suggest the first few steps to be taken when seeking to 'tap the industry channel' for reaching and helping a specific target group, such as women food processors.

1. Look carefully at all economically relevant backward and forward linkages of the target group; this should identify strong companies that might also benefit from improving the situation of the target group.
2. Approach these industries, requesting an exchange of views on possible industry–development co-operation. Usually marketing departments, demonstration departments, special projects officers or public relations officers, or (in smaller companies) the managing director, will be the best to approach.
3. Ask what the industry does in terms of the activities that might touch upon the target group. The industry may be in contact with the target group through its products, through its marketing campaigns, or through its distribution networks. It may provide inputs used by the target group, or itself use (raw) materials coming from the target group.
4. Brainstorm with the industry about possible ways to make the activities and objectives of industry and development overlap.
5. When concrete plans are taking shape, try to judge the effects of the plans on gender relations, and how the benefits will be dis-

tributed between the sexes. When plans are being carried out, monitor these aspects as well.

Summary and conclusions

This chapter has illustrated that market mechanisms can be a help for development workers promoting improved technologies, possibly resulting in a greater sustainability and a broader reach than development workers could achieve on their own. Although this approach is now gaining wider acceptance, so far almost no attention has yet been paid to its gender aspects. Yet it is particularly at this time, while the market-led approach is being further developed and tested, that it is essential to look into the gender issues of this approach.

Two forms of using market-driven mechanisms have been discussed. The first is to approach technology users as customers rather than as beneficiaries; a concrete way of doing this is to organize meetings between users and producers of tools in order to stimulate a user-led development and dissemination of improved technologies. The gender aspects of such meetings have been addressed. The more fundamental question of women's 'consumer power' leads to the need for insight into intra-household dynamics in order to discover the niches of women's autonomy. These niches form the entrance points for mobilizing women's 'consumer power'.

The second form of using market-driven mechanisms has been addressed in a more general way: the chapter discussed the possibility of using the resources of larger companies to achieve development objectives. While some risks are involved, the opportunities seem sufficiently worthwhile and should be added to the list of other ways to help men and women in farming, food processing and other activities. However, again it is not evident that such interventions will reach women as much as men. This can and should be monitored. Gender analysis instruments are available that can suggest the reasons and possible remedies for an uneven distribution of positive and negative effects.

Part Two
Engendering Development

5. Integrating gender in technological development

As described in the Preface, awareness of gender issues and women's needs can be divided into two main areas. First, there are activities that are specifically geared towards women (women's projects or women's components added on to general projects), and, second, there is the attempt to integrate gender concerns into general development activities. Attempts to introduce improved technologies to women's enterprises in an effective way, such as described in Chapters 2 and 3, are examples of the first area. The following chapters are mostly concerned with the latter area of activity: integrating gender into general development activities (that is, activities that do not have as their first specific aim the improvement of women's lives). This is known as 'mainstreaming gender'.

Mainstreaming gender into general development work has received an increasing degree of attention during the last decade (see Macdonald et al. 1997; Rao et al. 1991; Jahan 1995; Gianotten et al. 1994; Moser 1993). Attempts to mainstream gender also in *technology*-related projects are comparable to attempts in other domains of development, and similar issues will usually arise. However, some specific bottlenecks and needs come to the fore and have to be dealt with. This chapter describes a mainstreaming strategy aimed at achieving greater gender awareness and a more gender-inclusive practice in a (technical) development organization. It discusses in detail two aspects of the strategy: a gender analysis instrument and gender training. The strategy, instrument and training were developed for use in two organizations, TOOL and TOOLConsult, which are both organizations with their roots in the appropriate technology field.

Starting situation

The choice of mainstreaming approach is highly dependent on the situation existing before implementation. The starting situation of the organization and its employees should determine in which way gender issues are to be addressed. The approach described here is based on a starting situation which seems to exist in many Northern development organizations (and which, indeed, was present in the two organizations on which the approach described here was tried out), and which can be characterized as a situation of *basically positive but inactivated* attitudes.

In such a situation there is a relatively positive attitude towards gender issues. For example, most developments workers are aware that projects can fail if the role of women and the division of labour between men and women are not taken into account. Many people can cite an example of this, for example the famous case of a new water pump that was not used by the women because they preferred to continue walking to the well outside the village, this being their only opportunity for social interaction. Also, there is often awareness of the hardships of women, especially in the South. It no longer goes unnoticed how in some cultures men will spend much time drinking and conversing under the village tree while women are occupied working the land, cooking food, gaining an income, or doing any other of their myriad tasks.

Clearly, much of the attention paid to gender among general staff has been a result of pressure by donor institutions and by motivated individual (usually female) colleagues or employees. Thus, sometimes reluctantly, development staff attend gender training or write 'women paragraphs' into their project proposals. Objections to this are voiced, but often carefully: the general atmosphere is one where the importance of gender can no longer be denied.

Through this situation, many development staff have also developed a – usually somewhat scattered – basic knowledge of the position of women and of social differences between men and women. Most are aware, for instance, that women play an important role in agriculture, and know of the different spending patterns of men and women, the large number of women-headed households, or of women's limited access to resources resulting, for example, from inheritance laws and land-title laws.

However, the basic positive attitude and the scattered knowledge are very seldom put into practice in a regular and systematic way. This is what is meant by *inactivated*. The gender paragraphs written into project documents are usually not very impressive. The implementation of such gender paragraphs is usually even more disappointing. Above all, gender is not a priority; in situations of complexity and time pressure (quite normal in development work), serious attention to gender is the casualty.

Barriers A number of barriers can be identified that usually play a role in preventing a basically positive attitude from being put into practice in a systematic way. Just a few will be highlighted below.

Lack of understanding and disengagement There is often a lack of understanding of gender issues. For example, people will confuse 'having women on the staff' with 'taking women's needs into account'. Mostly, the word gender itself often remains mystifying even to people who have started to use it. Not without some knowledge of the subject, these people are often aware that they do not quite grasp some of the basics of the gender discussion. This can lead, especially among some men, to a fear of doing or saying something wrong and to a disengagement: a tendency to leave the thinking on gender to the gender expert.

Some of this fear and subsequent disengagement may be unintentionally enhanced by the gender and development world itself, which can have an exclusionary approach to the men who, admittedly, sometimes lag years behind in their knowledge, insight and openness to change regarding male–female relations. But if mainstreaming is the goal, rather than to convey the (ideologically important) intricacies and subtleties of the most recent phase of the gender debate, the challenge is to show that gender issues are on the one hand very easy and full of common sense, and at the same time complicated. It can then be stressed that anyone is able to grasp the common-sense parts of it and be responsible for bringing these into practice. For example, if the exact difference between 'women in development' and 'gender and development' is found difficult to grasp, a gender trainer can keep things simple for her trainees and just say that women must benefit from the trainees' development programmes. The subtleties and intricacies can then follow on from there. They will be linked more to practice and less to ideology.

Setting priorities As stated, the fear of doing it wrong can lead to a tendency to leave the gender work to the experts (or the women) among the staff. However, it is of course also easy to leave the work to the expert. Thus a degree of laziness, or priority setting, exacerbated in situations of time pressure, is also a barrier. To influence such priority setting, a strong and clear initiative from the side of management is indispensable.

Technical projects It is often more difficult to see the relevance of gender in technical projects than it is in projects that have an immediate social objective. In technical projects, the people are usually further away, and engineers are seldom trained to see the social aspects of their work. There is a divide between the technical and the social world. That technology has an impact on gender relations, and that gender relations help determine who will benefit from an 'improved' technology, are not easily seen by most engineers, except perhaps in terms of the idea that some tools would be too heavy or too large for women. This, in fact, is one of the least common gender-mitigated effects of technology.

A gender-integration trajectory

Elements of the gender-integration trajectory Because the barriers to gender integration are many and occur at different levels, gender integration cannot be achieved by one measure only. It is necessary to think in terms of something like a gender-integration trajectory, consisting of a number of different elements spread over a period of years. The main elements of a gender trajectory include:

- policy decisions by management
- group-wise training sessions for project staff
- individual advice and assistance on integrating gender in specific projects and activities
- choosing and adapting, or developing and testing an instrument for gender analysis of projects
- promoting the use of the gender instrument

Objective of the trajectory: basic gender capacity versus gender expertise The aim of a gender-integration trajectory is to create among the development staff of an organization both gender awareness and a capacity to integrate gender issues into general projects. The gender capacity of general staff, however, can be only on a basic level; not every staff member can become a gender specialist. In the final instance, gender issues are very complicated, and to improve the position of women through general projects – or even to avoid deterioration of their position – requires a thorough understanding of gender issues and a creative and concerted effort to deal with these issues.

However, there are also a number of rules or guidelines pertaining to gender that are quite simple and basic indeed. An important part of the problems that general projects create for women could be avoided if all development personnel at least possessed these basic insights and applied them to their daily work. Mainstreaming activities can be directed at this basic level. For the more intricate and fine-tuned gender activities, a gender expert remains necessary. One of the aims of instilling a basic gender capacity in general staff is to make them aware of the best time to call in a gender expert.

Discussing why an organization would aim for the integration of gender One of the objections to gender integration that frequently arise can be paraphrased as: 'How can we try to improve the position of women in our projects, when we already have so many other objectives to take care of as well? If we try to do everything at once we may end up not doing anything.'

This is a legitimate concern. Even in a situation such as in the Netherlands Department of Development (NEDA) – where one of the *general* objectives of development assistance is to empower women through all its activities taken together – it is probably not realistic, and may not be necessary, to make this an extra aim of every single development activity *separately*.

In order to structure the discussions and choices that can be made with regard to this question (Should every activity also aim at strengthening women?), the following overview has proved to be helpful. Almost always at a gender training, a discussion develops that can be clarified with this overview of objectives. It is also a strong tool for structuring discussions on an organization's gender policy.

The list below presents four possible motives for integrating gender issues into development work. Each successive objective in this overview is more extensive, or more 'radical' than the previous one. Strengthening the position of women is number four, the most far-reaching. The first motive is the 'instrumental' reason for integrating gender. Development staff are asked to discuss which of these objectives they themselves, or their organization, endorse.

Gender should be integrated in each project for the following reasons.

1. To achieve the original project objective (for instance, water supply, improved environment) more efficiently. In this approach, gender analysis is used only as a means, while improving the position of women need not be an objective. This is called an instrumental or efficiency approach.
2. To prevent the position of women from deteriorating in comparison with the situation before the project was initiated.
3. To prevent the position of women from deteriorating in comparison with the position of men. This aim implies that each project improving the position of men should equally improve the position of women. At the very least, projects carried out by an organization that mainly improve the position of men should be balanced by projects that mainly improve the position of women.
4. To improve gender relations (that is to say, to contribute to the empowerment of women).

NEDA officially endorses the fourth objective: the empowerment of women. Others may be prepared to aim only for the first or second objective. Few will denounce these objectives; indeed, it is very difficult to deny responsibility for taking gender into account for the reasons stated in these first two objectives. But even those who aim only at the first or second objective will usually need to intensify activities in the area of gender issues.

It does of course make a difference whether gender issues are considered for 'instrumental' reasons only (endorsement of objective 1 only), or to achieve empowerment for women (endorsement of objective 4). The instrumental arguments for gender integration have been much criticized from a feminist point of view. Therefore it is important to show that the different objectives will in specific instances lead to different choices, and in that sense can be conflicting. However, the general strategy of this exercise is to leave the participants free to choose the objective that they feel they can commit themselves to. It is not necessary to attempt to persuade participants to adopt the empowerment objective. Experience has shown that this exercise will generate enough useful discussion among the members of the organization themselves. Furthermore, in practice few participants will feel comfortable committing themselves to objective 1 only; objectives 2 and 3 just sound too reasonable. Also, the fact that an important donor demands objective 4 is a serious ground for discussion. But the most important outcome of this discussion is that, as long as participants agree with at least objective 1 and/or 2 (and few will not), even just that usually means that a great amount of gender-integration work still needs to be done.

The 'EGA' or Efficient Gender Analysis instrument

It seems possible partly to address the barriers to achieving a practice of gender integration through the introduction of practical, user-friendly and efficient gender analysis instruments. With this in mind, such an analysis instrument was developed by the author for use in TOOL and TOOLConsult and elsewhere. With this instrument, called the EGA (Efficient Gender Analysis), any planned or existing project can be systematically examined in order to find out whether women will benefit from it as much as men, and to generate recommendations to improve the project in this respect.

The EGA instrument is based on one that was at the time being developed by NEDA (Lingen 1994), but differs from it on a number of important points. The main characteristics of the EGA are:

- The EGA can be used by staff members with no particular expertise in the area of gender issues.
- The EGA can be carried out in any phase of the project cycle. Specific instructions are provided for each phase.
- The EGA is time-efficient and concise, which makes it a suitable tool for frequent use.
- The EGA requires a minimal time investment, so it can be used for both large programmes and small projects.
- The EGA can be carried out on the basis of project documents, interim or final evaluations and/or oral accounts by local experts.

- The EGA makes a gender analysis of a *project or programme*. This may subsequently lead to the conclusion that a gender analysis of the *target group* is also needed, which will produce information on the distribution of tasks and resources among the men and women of the target group. This sequence, where the project is taken as a starting point, makes it easier for the project staff to see the relevance of subsequent target group analyses.

The objective of the EGA: recommendations The main objective of the EGA is to formulate recommendations aimed at improving the integration of gender aspects in a planned or ongoing project At the end of the analysis, the recommendations should be prioritized, and at least some should be selected to be carried out.

EGA is thus not primarily aimed at labelling projects as either gender-sensitive or gender-insensitive, although the information acquired by means of an EGA often gives a general idea of the level of gender-sensitivity of a project. There is, however, no direct correlation between the number of recommendations generated by the EGA and the level of gender-sensitivity of a project. For example, a highly gender-sensitive project could yield numerous recommendations for further improvement, while a project that pays little attention to gender may give rise to one recommendation only. After the first recommendation has been carried out, a second Efficient Gender Analysis may yield many more recommendations.

Overview of the EGA The EGA consists of three parts: an analysis of the *objectives* of a project or programme; an analysis of the *planned* or *realized activities*; and an analysis of the planned or expected *outputs and effects* of the project. Each part consists of a number of questions, which should be answered with a few sentences. The questions should in the first instance be answered with the knowledge that project officers already have with regard to the project situation, and by using the existing project documents, ToRs, interim evaluations, mission reports and strategy documents. Most information will be in these documents, but the analysts must be able to read between the lines, as the desired information is not always stated explicitly. Often, oral reports can be used to supplement written documentation. For some questions, it may be necessary to commission a third party to perform a gender analysis of the target group.

One of the first and central steps in the EGA is to reformulate the objectives of a project in such a way that women become visible as a target group (see 1.3 in the overview below). Women are often targeted implicitly, but to make the EGA analysis possible, women must be named explicitly. For example, when the project objective is 'to introduce biogas technology to the village community', women can be made visible by reformulating this objective as follows: 'to introduce biogas technology in such a way that both men and women from the village community benefit from this introduction'. This simple reformulation makes it possible to ask questions about the activities that the project carries out; these activities are questioned in the second part of the EGA. For example (see question 2.1): are the activities that are planned for the biogas project adequate, not only to introduce biogas, but also to 'introduce biogas in such a way that also women will benefit'?

The following box gives an overview of the EGA questions. The full manual contains explanations, tips and examples for each of these questions.

Part 1: EGA on the objectives of the project

1.1 Are the objectives of the project gender-specific?
1.2 If so, does the project also aim at supporting women's empowerment?
   • Formulate recommendations.
1.3 Assume that the objectives are implicitly gender-inclusive, and make these objectives explicit where relevant.
   • Formulate recommendations.
1.4 What implicit gender-selectivity can be expected in this project, given the definition of the *target group*?
   • Formulate recommendations.
1.5 To what extent does the project address the needs of women?
   • Formulate recommendations.

Part 2: EGA on project approach

2.1 Are the project *strategy or approach* and the planned or realized *activities* appropriate for achieving the objectives of the project in a gender-inclusive manner?

- Formulate recommendations.

2.2 Are adequate *budget, personnel and other inputs* available?
- Formulate recommendations.

2.3 Are the *institutional conditions* appropriate?
- Formulate recommendations.

2.4 What is the expected participation of women in the various phases of the project cycle?
- Formulate recommendations.

2.5 Analyse the project documentation for implicit assumptions regarding gender relations. Are these assumptions correct?
- Formulate recommendations.

Part 3: EGA on outputs and effects of the project

3.1 How are the gender-inclusive objectives reflected in the planned outputs?
- Formulate recommendations.

3.2 How are these objectives translated into indicators of success or indicators for monitoring and evaluation?
- Formulate recommendations.

3.3 What are the expected positive or negative effects of the project for women (with respect to gender relations and women's autonomy)
- Formulate recommendations.

Finally

Compare the recommendations formulated on the basis of the above questions. Now select, on the basis of their importance and feasibility, one or more recommendations to be implemented in the next phase of the project.

EGA for small projects The EGA can be used for both large programmes and small projects. There is no reason for excluding projects from an EGA on the basis of their small size or short duration. A short project, for example an identification mission, may have serious implications if insufficient attention is paid to gender aspects. It would therefore be useful to include a number of guidelines on gender-sensitivity in the ToR. These can be formulated by means of an EGA. After some practice, it should be possible to perform a global gender analysis of a small project in two to three hours.

The more complex a project or programme is, the more time-intensive the EGA will be. For example, a project with many different components and objectives requires an EGA for each separate component. However, even the analysis of a large and complex project with EGA need not take more than one or two days. This means that if an EGA is carried out about once a year, the time spent on analysis will be small in proportion to the total project time. Of course, the serious implementation of the recommendations generated is not so easily done.

EGA for 'indirect' projects The EGA can also be used to analyse projects that do not seem to involve people at all, and certainly do not seem to have any gender aspects. This is often the case with technical projects, which involve the transfer of hardware and the development of a technical infrastructure, and which are not immediately directed at people. An example would be 'Twinning for Electricity Companies', a project implemented by TOOLConsult in which a Dutch regional energy company and the Indian Karnataka Electricity Board co-operated to improve the efficiency and reliability of energy distribution. Even in these types of projects (which can be called 'indirect projects') an EGA can be carried out, but this requires a somewhat different approach.

For example, EGA point 1.3 asks the analyst to 'Assume that the objectives are implicitly gender-inclusive, and make these gender objectives explicit where relevant.' When a project is aimed (to continue the example above) at processes and techniques in electricity companies, men, women and gender differences are hardly relevant in a direct sense and are not directly affected by the project (although the results of the project may have some effect on the employees of the electricity companies). Thus it may seem impossible and irrelevant to make gender aspects explicit as the question asks. However, even 'indirect' projects are based on the general idea that they will contribute to the well-being of people; this can be seen as the underlying objective of such a project. When analysing the project objectives of an indirect project, we should focus therefore on such objectives as lie behind the immediate project objectives. In the underlying objectives, the relevance of gender is usually much more clear. Three questions structure this analysis of the objectives of indirect projects:

1. What kind of improvements in the well-being of people form the underlying aims of this project?
2. What could be the reasons why this might apply less to women than to men?
3. Are there any possible negative effects for women?

In the example of the twinning project mentioned above, the project document states that the project wants to contribute to a number of underlying objectives. (Although they are not listed as such exactly, the general motivation and rationale of the project use them as arguments.) The underlying objectives are: (a) greater reliability of the electricity supply; (b) savings on investments; (c) savings on fossil fuels; and (d) ongoing electrification of India.

The EGA thus leads, among others, to the question of to what extent women benefit from a more reliable and more widely available electricity grid. The answer to this question may be that not enough is known about it. In that case, the relevant recommendation could be that an organization that does many projects on rural electrification should undertake some research into this question: for example, to write this research into a project proposal or to suggest it as additional activity for an existing project.

The EGA in practice: both analysis and dialogue instrument The EGA can take from two to eight hours to carry out, depending on the character of the project and the thoroughness of the analysis. The EGA should preferably be carried out every twelve to eighteen months, to incorporate the changes that occur during implementation, and to judge the gender effects of any discrepancies that arise between a project plan and the way the project is actually carried out.

EGAs were carried out by non-gender experts from TOOL and TOOLConsult. Although there was some initial reluctance, all staff members were able to carry out the EGA in a meaningful way. The sophistication of the analyses differed, but all EGAs generated at least some recommendations for improvement of the gender aspects of the analysed project. Staff members generally found that the tool helped them in judging the gender effects of their projects.

However, the EGA has been found to be particularly effective when it is used as a dialogue instrument in an organization. In this set-up, the gender expert analyses a number of the (most recent) projects of an organization. This will lead to the identification of strong points and recommendations for improvements. This is done in close dialogue with the staff member responsible for the project, who should have information about the project and its target groups. The gender expert channels this information in such a way that it generates the needed information on gender aspects of the project. Thus, when used as a dialogue instrument, the EGAs are done by the gender expert and the project staff together.

Used in this way, the EGA is at one and the same time an instrument for analysis, and an instrument for training and awareness creation. After a few such exercises where project leader and gender expert work together, the project leader can usually undertake future EGAs independently.

The training

Another part of the gender-integration trajectory is a training session or, better, a series of training sessions to be combined either in a concentrated two or three days, or spread over time.

Objectives of the training   The objectives of the training are to increase the gender awareness of the project staff, to increase their ability to integrate gender aspects into their activities, and to instil or activate the necessary knowledge about gender. More specifically, it aims to achieve the following situation:

- Participants are aware of the need to integrate gender in their work.
- Participants have global knowledge of the situation of women and gender relations in different cultural contexts.
- Participants know how and where to get additional information on women and gender relations in different cultural contexts.
- Participants can analyse projects with regard to gender aspects.
- Participants can generate recommendations for improving projects with regard to gender.

Overview of the training   The three main aspects of the training are awareness, skills and knowledge, and the three training modules each address one of these. The model below reflects the way the three modules are linked together, and how they are aimed at influencing, on the one hand, attitudes (gender awareness), and, on the other hand, action (capacity to integrate gender).[1] Module 1 is directly aimed at gender awareness; Module 2 teaches the participants the skills to use instruments to integrate gender in their work. Module 2 also contributes indirectly to gender awareness, and Module 3, while it addresses knowledge, also contributes to gender integration skills and, through Module 2, gender awareness.

Model of the training

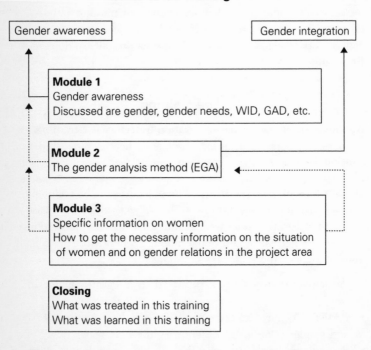

Gender awareness Gender awareness is addressed most directly in Module 1. After an introduction to the training, the importance of gender is illustrated through examples of development projects. Atten-

---

1. This model was developed by Mariska Schurink, who did practical work for her master's degree on the gender training.

tion is also paid to the concepts 'gender', 'women in development' (WID), 'gender and development' (GAD), strategic and practical gender needs and the three roles of women (see also the Preface).

Discussing the meaning of gender Before a definition of gender is given, participants are asked to brainstorm and decide for themselves what gender is all about. Rather than emphasize an exact definition, the module looks at characteristics of the concept of gender: what does it in any case have to do with? The following definition of gender is then presented: '*Gender* is the cultural pattern of differentiation between men and women.' It is stressed that the pattern of differentiation between men and women will be different depending on the culture, but that all cultures do have such a pattern. The differentiation is reflected in the different roles and tasks of men and women, their different degrees of access to resources, and their different identities. Moreover, differentiation is almost never a neutral inequality, but also *inequity* in the sense that women as a group have fewer options, less power, status and access to resources than men. Gender, moreover, is not the only cultural pattern of differentiation that exists within cultures. Race, caste and age are some of the others.

Women versus gender About ten years ago, it became commonplace to speak of 'gender' rather than of 'women'. This change must be addressed in gender training. The present training mainly intends to demystify the change by presenting the account in the following box.

From women to gender to women

Women The first awareness of the position of women in development arose when it was noticed that women as a group are in many respects disadvantaged *vis-à-vis* men, and that the situation of women often deteriorates (relatively) as a result of development interventions. This is in fact always the issue behind any awareness of 'gender' or 'women'.

No women without gender In the years following, it was realized that, in order to understand the situation, and especially the disadvantaged situation, of women, we have to understand *gender*, the cultural pattern of differentiation between men and women. Also, it is not possible to improve the situation of women without being aware of the way gender influences women's opportunities.

It became less usual to say that 'one should also look at the role of women' when planning activities, and more usual to say that 'gender should be taken into account'. Rather than say 'we want to improve the situation of women', we could say 'we want to make gender relations more egalitarian'.

Next to women, the term gender brings men into view. It specifically directs attention to the interaction and power relations between men and women. It brings into the picture all the factors that together form and sustain gender relations, such as: men, women, institutions, law, religion, art, education, etc.

No egalitarian gender relations without strengthening women Gender is about women and men. But the inequality in gender relations can often be addressed by strengthening the position of *women* and fulfilling the needs of *women*. This is because the inequality almost always means that women are worse off.

So, from gender, we very often come back to women: projects for women, identifying the needs of women. But now it is realized that women's possibilities and needs are strongly determined by gender. One way to show and to remember this is to speak of 'gender needs' rather than 'women's needs'.

Practical gender needs versus strategic gender needs Moser makes a distinction between *practical* and *strategic* gender needs. Although in practice it is not very easy to determine whether a specific need is either practical or strategic, the distinction is often useful for trainees. In the present training, participants work from a case description to identify the practical and strategic needs. Practical gender needs are the needs women have *given their specific gender role*. Strategic gender needs are needs that challenge the gender roles. Projects that focus only on addressing practical needs leave the division of roles and the power balance between men and women unchallenged. For example, if women are taught how to prepare better and more nourishing meals, a practical need is addressed. But the assumption that women are responsible for feeding their families and taking care of their general well-being is accepted, and even reconfirmed. However, if a project is also aimed at helping women to achieve more control over household finances, a strategic gender need (i.e. empowerment) is involved.

Gender integration skills A substantial part of the training is directed at analysing projects with the EGA. All main aspects of the EGA are explained and in a series of exercises participants are made comfortable with the method. In all exercises, cases are used from the project portfolios of the participants themselves.

It is stressed that the main purpose of any gender analysis of a project is to get an answer to the following questions:

- Will women benefit from this project?
- How could this be improved if necessary?
- Could there be unintended negative effects for women?
- If so how could these be avoided or compensated for?

To answer these questions we must, on the one hand, look at the project (for example, with the EGA), at its objectives, its target group, its activities and the way it monitors and evaluates its results. On the other hand, it is necessary to know enough about the gender situation in the relevant region. The questions of knowledge about the gender situation are addressed in the third module.

Knowledge In the process of doing an EGA, the need will almost always arise to find out more about gender in the specific context of the project situation. This experienced need is taken as the starting point for the module on information on women and gender relations. Two kinds of information or knowledge are distinguished. The first kind is a rather general knowledge of the characteristics of the position of women and of gender relations that tend to be true in most societies. This general kind of knowledge is a very helpful starting point when carrying out an Efficient Gender Analysis: it shows the analyst at least some of the points where a project might start to cause problems for women, or end up being irrelevant to them. Most development workers who read the general journals and papers on development (and do not systematically skip the articles on gender) will have some knowledge on this general level; often more than they realize. To bring this out, participants in the training are presented with a list of general tendencies regarding gender, and are asked to continue the list based on their directly available knowledge.

The second level of knowledge concerns detailed knowledge of the specific situation of the project's target group. This is the kind of knowledge that no one has readily available for more than one or two projects, because where the details of gender relations are concerned, every project situation is different. While in the first section on information, participants were shown that they may already know more than they realize, in this section it is made clear that this knowledge is never enough to be sure of the specific project situation. This is not because of their inadequacy but stems from the fact that gender relations are so site- and time-specific. While general gender knowledge is immensely important for basic insights into the gender aspects of a project, further knowledge on the field level is almost always required.

Referring back to the main questions which form the background of a gender analysis, participants are asked to answer the following questions:

- What else do you need to know (about women and gender relations) to be able to judge whether women will be among the project beneficiaries and whether the project addresses their needs?
- What do you need to know to be able to formulate ways to improve the project from the point of view of gender?
- What do you need to know to be able to estimate possible unintended negative effects for women?
- What do you need to know to be able to find ways to avoid and compensate for such negative effects?

Based on the answers to these questions, participants are asked to formulate a 'Terms of Reference', specifying the information that still needs to be gathered by a gender specialist.

Conclusion: rules of a gender-integration trajectory

A gender-integration trajectory can benefit from by and large adhering to a number of general rules. These rules are relevant for organizations with a starting situation as described above, character-ized by 'basically positive but inactivated' attitudes. They intend to make the most of the positive elements of this starting situation, while addressing the gaps. The rules are:

1. Address practice, not attitudes.
2. Approach people in a positive way: presuppose a willingness to increase attention for gender.
3. Illuminate and work with what people already know about gender.
4. Present simple tools that are used, rather than perfect ones which are not used. The tools should be pragmatic and time-efficient.
5. Work both top-down (get clear commitment from management) and bottom-up (training, tools and direct advice for all personnel).
6. Work towards a basic gender expertise for everyone. But keep in mind that not everyone can and needs to be a gender expert.

With these rules in mind, a gender-integration trajectory should be carried out on different levels and in different ways at the same time, including training, advice, policy and instruments. It is not a one-time activity, and at least several years of constant and repeated effort will be required to change a situation with basically positive but inactivated attitudes into one where gender considerations are systematically and naturally integrated into the full spectrum of considerations leading up to development initiatives.

6. 'Let's do gender today': gender awareness training for engineers

Marie C. Fry

During the past six years the author of this chapter has been developing gender-training materials for agricultural engineers and scientists in Bangladesh and for water and irrigation engineers in Vietnam. In both cases these engineers and scientists had no previous training in sociology or any education in the humanities. It was interesting to note that, at the beginning the project, managers were of the opinion that a nod to gender could be done in a half-day session (in one case in a one-hour session!), but that in the event they came to see attention to gender issues as fundamental to the overall success of the project. The now conventional gender-planning strategy of carefully selecting the right 'entry point' (that is, going through the appropriate management level) was crucial in both cases. The preparation and planning with the managers, and the introduction of the topic to them, was as much a part of the training programme as the actual course preparation and delivery.

Bangladesh

The brief for the gender training in Bangladesh was to introduce gender issues to the Department of Agricultural Extension (DAE) of the Ministry of Agriculture. There were approximately 2,000 diploma or graduate staff at the headquarters with qualifications in one of the agricultural sciences or agricultural engineering. Next to these, there were 14,000 field staff with varying levels of education from diploma to school-leaving certificate supported by on the job training. The field staff were organized in a block system and one day each month was allocated for training.

All the diploma and graduate staff at the headquarters had been educated within the narrow focus of their specialist subject, and some 1,200 of them held the job title 'subject matter specialist'. Of the total number of staff, approximately sixty were women, all working in a marginalized department entitled 'Homestead Gardening'. The DAE was a hierarchical organization, where qualification and length of time in post were the key to future advancement, and where women were marginalized and separated from the mainstream of the organization. It was not therefore an atmosphere conducive to change. To bring about change in the form of gender awareness in such a large rigid organization was a daunting task, and the only impetus for any attempt at change was the requirement of the funding agency that gender be incorporated into a project titled 'Agricultural Support Services', which was aimed at the upgrading, rationalization and development of the DAE. It was a clear case of outside forces influencing local policy.

Such a large task called for limited objectives. The raising of the level of awareness was the best that could be hoped for in the first phase of the project, and the process of developing awareness had to begin at the top of the organization. A symposium aimed at enabling senior management to introduce gender to the organization was arranged. It was crucial that this was attended by the director-general and his senior staff, of whom there were approximately twelve, and that a significant amount of time was allocated for it. In the event, a one-day symposium was organized and the director-general attended for approximately one-third of the time, just enough to give it credibility in the eyes of the rest of the staff. At the symposium, the author gave a paper on the need for gender awareness in the Agricultural Extension Department in Bangladesh, with examples and case studies. Approximately half of the time was allocated for group work and group discussion, as it was important that the participants worked out the arguments for themselves, and did not simply attend another lecture. At the end of the symposium the director-general recommended that a similar one-day training be organized for the next level of senior staff, of whom there were about 220, and that trainers should be identified who would, after suitable preparation, be able to train the field staff. The one-day training became a two-day training programme for senior staff, and a training course and materials were developed for use by the trainers who would subsequently train all the district staff who would in turn train the 14,000 field staff members.

Given the commitment of senior management, the next phase was relatively easy to organize in logistical terms, but the questions of how to approach the topic, what form the training should take, and what materials to use remained. The participative training method was chosen and a programme devised which led the participants through a series of questions, leading to a set of conclusions and action points.

The programme of training was organized into three distinct parts:

- A two-day gender-awareness programme for senior staff at headquarters and in each of the twenty-four districts, called the Gender Responsive Extension Programming (GREP) course.
- A training of trainers programme for the staff from the training unit who had been selected as gender trainers (twenty-four in all), called the GREP-TOT. The trainers were all male, and were selected from those who had expressed an interest in the subject. The training of trainers programme was a four-day classroom-based programme plus one day of practice teaching in the field.
- A basic two-day gender-awareness course for the trainers to teach to the rest of the district staff who in turn could teach it to the remaining staff in the field.

A two-day course in Gender Responsive Extension Programming   The rationale for the two-day GREP training for the specialist engineers was that it should look as scientific as possible, that every statistic and figure quoted was referenced and quantified, and that the sociology was set out in short numbered points leading to a general conclusion. This is somewhat different from academic sociology and the author's non-sociological background was probably a help rather than a hindrance here.

The programme had to address five main issues, which were in order of priority:

- cultural and religious norms which meant that male extension staff were not easily able to speak to women clients

- subject-matter specializations which led people to a very narrow approach to agriculture, when what rural women in Bangladesh needed was a much broader approach encompassing issues such as water and fuel and health
- the extremely low status of rural women, and the fact that almost all previous activity had concentrated on homestead gardening for women as the sole extension route
- gender roles in the rural areas were perceived as rigidly defined, and literacy rates for both adult and young females were very low in comparison to the already low rates for males
- women's use of technology was minimal, and the introduction of more suitable technologies was a key part of the project rationale

It was immediately clear that new materials would have to be created, and that the course design would need to incorporate an enormous amount of information into a relatively short period of time. It is interesting to note that there was a wealth of reports and statistical material available which had never been analysed from a gender perspective; also material from the NGO sector was in many cases dis-aggregated by sex. What evolved was a two-day programme of gender-awareness raising which was highly participative, used a number of illustrative case studies – mainly but not exclusively from the Bangladesh agricultural sector – and concluded with a personal action plan for each participant. Although the programme was highly participative, and used brainstorming group work and discussion as its main pedagogical methods, the materials which the participants took away with them had to be factually accurate and easy to use and to read.

The course was divided into four modules each lasting half a day. In the box on p. 110 the objectives of each module are given.

The first task in the training was to look at women's and men's work and to try to make the linkages between the production of food and its processing and preparation. The attendant needs for water and fuel emerged as natural parts of this exercise. This exercise often produced much hilarity, but provided a useful antidote to what many had anticipated as training about 'women's rights'. Having established the linkages between women's and men's work it was time to look at their roles within society. This provided an opportunity to look at the basic sociological definitions of society and community,

Module title	After completing this module each participant will be able to:
1. Understanding the issues	• identify accurately female and male tasks • understand the connections between tasks in the field and in the homestead • relate field and homestead activities to the farming system • understand how the work of all household members is connected • understand how farm incomes are constructed • understand how the work of each household member contributes to farm income
2. Relating issues and people	• relate tasks to individuals • understand how information is transmitted between people • understand the importance of giving information to the person who does the task • be able to describe and define the 'new clients' i.e. women • make suitable suggestions for targeting the 'new clients'
3. Targeting for improvements	• describe how the homestead operates • describe the technologies women already use • understand the constraints on women and how those constraints govern women's work • identify activities which could make the homestead more productive • identify target activities which could increase income
4. Selecting methods and technologies	• describe alternative extension methods available • select appropriate alternative extension methods for working with women • relate methods to targeted technologies • select suitable technologies for increasing income • define the key issues to be considered in selecting methods and technologies to increase farm incomes

and reinforced the mutuality of life in rural Bangladesh. For this purpose, a bit of instant sociology was applied and packaged in a format acceptable to all participants, some of whom soon began to see themselves as 'agricultural sociologists' in their search for a new hierarchy. At the second stage the crucial definition of gender could now be made and within that premise the analysis of gender needs and strategic and practical interests could be introduced. All this was constantly related back to the participants' own analysis of women's and men's work and roles in society. The third stage was to look at the constraints and to search for ways to overcome them, and the fourth stage was to create gender-aware plans for each of the participants' jobs.

A five-day training of trainers (TOT) course The second course that was developed was the TOT course. This consisted of six three-and-a-half-hour modules designed to run immediately after the Gender Responsive Extension Programming course, making a five-day training programme in total. This GREP-TOT course focused on the rationale for gender-responsive extension programming as well as the methodologies suitable for gender-aware training. It aimed to:

- help trainers of the Department of Agricultural Extension (DAE) to deliver the GREP course effectively to a wide range of DAE staff
- give selected DAE trainers increased competence in gender issues and in gender-aware training
- provide DAE trainers with a range of suitable materials for adaptation and use at all levels of the service

In addition to the GREP described above, the following subjects were covered:

Day 1: *Relating gender issues to DAE and agriculture in Bangladesh, and becoming familiar with the training methods and the materials*

- understanding participatory training methods
- government and DAE policy on gender
- how DAE work is related to national policy on gender
- the concept of gender as it relates to Bangladesh and agriculture
- training methods used for the GREP course

- using transparencies and handouts

Day 2: *Gender and technology issues and relating course materials to audience*
- the 'triple role' of women
- technology and homestead productivity
- social, welfare and productive technologies
- implementing homestead technologies: questions to be asked
- constructing a checklist for suitability of technologies for homestead use
- relating TOT and GREP materials and concepts
- using the materials
- adapting and simplifying the materials.

Day 3: *Practical training sessions with peer group*
- preparing a script using the trainer's notes and other materials
- delivering a session to peer group
- assessment and evaluation

The objectives of each of the six extra modules of the TOT course are listed the following box.

Module title	After completing this module each participant will be able to:
1. Relating gender issues to DAE and agriculture in Bangladesh	• understand participatory training methods • describe and explain government policy on gender • explain how DAE work is related to national policy on gender • define and explain the concept of gender as it relates to agriculture and technology in Bangladesh
2. Training methods and practice	• be familiar with the training methods used for the course and understand how to use them • be able to demonstrate the use of overhead transparencies and handouts in the context of the GREP course

3. Gender and techno- logy issues	• describe and explain the 'triple role' of women • explain how technology can help to improve the productivity of the homestead and contribute to household income • define and explain social, welfare and productive technologies • define the questions to be asked before implementing homestead technologies • be able to construct a checklist for defining suitable technologies for homestead use
4. Relating the course materials to the audience	• relate the TOT materials and the materials for the GREP course • be familiar with the material for both courses and keep it in an accessible form • simplify and adapt materials to meet audience needs
5. Preparing training sessions	• be capable of preparing a suitable script using the trainers' notes and other materials to teach the GREP course
6. Practice in teaching the GREP course	• have delivered a session of the course with confidence • have gained confidence in using the materials provided • understand the criteria by which peer group assessment is made

This course was supported with background reading, overhead projector slides, photographic slides, trainers' notes, lesson plans and handouts. A twelve-page course booklet was also prepared with a page each on the nature of society, women's and men's roles in society, gender terminology, gender planning outline, extension methodologies and communication methods.

Vietnam

A similar project was undertaken in Vietnam in 1996, this time for irrigation and hydraulics engineers. Once again the low status of women, lack of suitable technologies and an insensitive gender climate were the main issues, and awareness-raising and sensitization were the best outcomes that could be hoped for. The project was titled 'Capacity Building in the Water Resources Sector', and its aim was to upgrade existing irrigation schemes and to strengthen the indigenous staff's ability to develop new schemes. Here again, the crucial driving factor was that gender was built into the project specification by the donors. However, the main constraint to the integration of gender concerns was the language used to define and describe the project. General phrases such as 'capacity building' and 'public participation' can obscure the need for paying attention especially to women, particularly in countries where neither 'public' nor 'participation' necessarily includes women. The immediate questions that come to mind from the point of view of gender are: 'Whose capacity?', 'Whose participation?' and 'Who is part of the water resources sector?' While a gender-sensitive interpretation of general terminology is obvious to those who are gender-aware, the reality is that many project staff are not gender-aware and such phrases do not automatically lead them to include women. Thus, although gender issues were specified in the project appraisal documents, it would have been all too easy *almost* to ignore them or to pay only the slightest attention to them.

In the case of the Vietnam project, the chosen method of capacity building and developing public participation in the water sector was a six-week TOT course in the UK at the Southampton Institute of Irrigation Studies, with training materials developed to be used with irrigation staff training in Vietnam. One component of the six-week course was a two-day programme on gender awareness-raising using participatory methods. The concept of gender was entirely new to the trainers, and there was the added complication of translation into Vietnamese, a language in which there is no direct translation for the word 'gender' and in which pronouns are not sex-specific, thus the possibility of distortion was always present. In the event, two of the trainers were relatively fluent in English and a reasonable compromise seems to have been reached.

On the basis of this TOT programme in the UK, the Vietnamese trainers delivered the two-day course to the engineering staff of the Vietnamese Institute of Hydraulics Engineering in Hanoi. The author travelled to Vietnam to assist the trainers in delivering the first of the gender sessions. The programme of the two-day course, which was prepared in collaboration with the Vietnamese trainers, included the following modules:

- introduction to public participation in development
- social issues involved in achieving participation of all members of society
- stakeholder and group identification
- costs and benefits of participation to different members of the community.

The starting point for the gender-awareness raising was a series of questions: Who are the public? What constitutes the community? What is a group? Who participates? Who are the stakeholders? Why are they stakeholders? This was followed by an analysis of women's and men's tasks, and then the subject of participation and methods of participation were related to the time available for everyone. Daily time-use charts and seasonal analyses were shown to be crucial in providing the 'evidence' for decision-making.

The final exercise of the Vietnamese gender training for irrigation and hydraulics engineers was a costs and benefits exercise. The course participants were asked to 'think about the social relationships in Vietnam', and – taking into account all the evidence accumulated about the differing roles of women and men – to make a table of what the costs and benefits of an improved irrigation system *might* be to women and men.

The box on p. 116 shows one of the tables produced by a group of four men and one woman.

The course was designed with lesson plans, and supporting materials such as overhead projector slides, handouts and background reading. The course participants were encouraged to keep their own folders with notes on group discussions and brainstorming sessions, and to compare group checklists against a standard set prepared by the trainers.

Benefits to women	Costs to women	Benefits to men	Costs to men
Water may be more easily available, saving time in fetching water, and possibly the burden of carrying it.	Increased land in production can mean more weeding which is usually women's work, also more harvesting and threshing (also women's work).	Increased land in production means more income, which he may or may not share with his wife.	Increased land in production means more inputs, more ploughing and possibly purchase of machinery.
Participation in women's groups is empowering for women and helps them to develop skills such as leadership and literacy.	Participation takes time, which is a major constraint for women.	Participation in groups is empowering to men and develops other skills such as leadership.	Participation takes time and although men usually have more leisure time than women, they still have to travel to meetings and therefore be away from farm activities.
Participation in women's groups leads to a wider participation in committees and councils.	The cost of travelling to participate in a wider sphere is often a constraint for women.	Increased income means increased ability to buy goods and services.	Part of the increased income may have to be spent on servicing loans.
Increased money in the family should lead to increased opportunities to buy goods and services.	Women's field work is most often unpaid; women may therefore simply have more work but no financial benefit.		
	Part of the increased income may have to be spent on servicing loans.		

Conclusions

From the two experiences discussed above, it is possible to draw the following broad conclusions:

- It is important for donors and project designers to include gender as a mandatory part of any project.
- The project appraisal language has an increasing tendency to generalize and is in danger of obscuring women in the assumption that the words 'public' and 'participation' automatically include women in the minds of engineers.
- Many engineers have a very narrow specialist focus, and they need to see gender as an important issue in terms of their career and qualifications as well as in terms of equity between women and men.
- It is important that men are intellectually engaged in gender issues, not simply as course participants, but as gender trainers as well.
- Time allocated for gender is always extremely limited so that usually only awareness raising is possible in the short time available.
- Examples and case studies need to be taken from the relevant sectors of science or engineering.
- Statistics and examples need to be properly referenced and the topic should be presented in as scientific a way as possible.
- The project rationale and project documents specifying gender and country gender policy need to be quoted and referenced.
- The possibility of dilution and distortion is always present when such large numbers are being trained, and a strong quality control mechanism is of prime importance.

7. 'Making each and every farmer count': gender and participation in agricultural engineering projects

Megan Lloyd-Laney, Josef Kienzle and Saskia Everts

Agricultural sector programmes and policies, extension services, as well as designers of agricultural tools and equipment, have generally ignored women farmers' needs and concerns and their important contribution to agricultural production and rural economy. Yet according to IFAD (the International Fund for Agricultural Development), in many African countries, women provide 90 per cent of the hoeing and weeding field work; 70 per cent of the agricultural work; 80 per cent of food storage and transport from farm to village; and they do 100 per cent of the processing for basic foodstuffs. Hence, women use agricultural tools and equipment in their daily life and are therefore important clients for the agricultural engineering sector, and their needs should be more carefully considered and incorporated in project planning (FAO 1990; 1997).

To increase the awareness of gender issues among its staff, the agricultural engineering branch of the FAO (Food and Agriculture Organization) is implementing a sub-programme on gender issues. A specific feature of the programme is an attempt also to look through the eyes of the agricultural engineers themselves. What is their perception of 'integrating gender issues'? What are the barriers that keep them from considering gender issues? What could prompt them to integrate a concern for women's need into their work? The pro-gramme has so far included three main activities:

- a workshop on gender and agricultural engineering where gender experts and agricultural engineers mainly from southern and east-ern Africa met to exchange views
- a series of interviews with male and female agricultural engineers, also from southern and eastern Africa
- the production of a booklet intended to familiarize engineers with reasons and ways to integrate gender

In all three activities, the agricultural engineering section of the FAO (AGSE) worked in close co-operation with the SIDA-funded FAO field programme FARMESA (Farm-level Applied Research Methods for East and Southern Africa).

Target group

Nowadays there is some training material and literature available for those individuals and institutions who are already aware that gender needs must be taken into consideration and want to be assisted in how to do this (e.g. Feldstein et al. 1994; Parker 1993; Thomas-Slayter et al. 1995; Williams et al. 1994). However, there is a large group of people in key positions in agricultural engineering that is not so convinced that gender is an issue, or that gender considerations need to be integrated in project planning. The gender activities of AGSE and FARMESA were designed to address this latter group. Specifically, three groups of people formed the target group:

- middle- and senior-level agricultural engineers working in the ministries
- university academics working in the agricultural field, both in curriculum development and as researchers and consultants
- project practitioners, for example personnel working within non-governmental organizations, in charge of agricultural projects

The last thing that these busy, senior and experienced practitioners want is another lecture on how important it is for them to be 'gender aware' in their work. Most of them do not care much about the involvement and participation of women farmers *per se*, but they do care about helping farmers: helping them to increase productivity, to lessen their burden of work, to increase the range of farming options, and to optimize the current farming system. If these objectives can be better achieved by reaching women and recognizing gender issues, then that is a much more convincing reason to include women and gender than simply addressing gender issues for their own sake. Thus, in the AGSE programme a non-confrontational and 'instrumental' (as described in Chapter 5) approach seemed to be called for.

Workshop

In March 1996 a workshop was held in Kadoma organized by AGSE and the AGROTEC project (the predecessor of FARMESA). The following description draws upon the report of the workshop by Schoemaker and Jassey (1996).

The workshop was attended by thirty-five participants, about two-thirds of whom were engineers involved in equipment design and formulation and implementation of practical development projects, while the others were persons with a gender or WID background. The workshop was, on the one hand, designed to increase awareness of gender among its participants, but on the other hand, and more importantly, it was a place and occasion where social scientists could learn from engineers who were strongly involved in agricultural engineering. For example, they could see how engineers currently considered and dealt with social and gender issues. The workshop was therefore an occasion to generate ideas on how FAO and other organizations should deal with gender in agricultural engineering.

Programme The workshop methodology was a combination of presentations (keynote papers and country case studies), plenary discussions and working group sessions. In addition, a 'market day' was organized where participants were able to provide inputs such as presentations, information material and videos as well as ideas for the rest of the workshop programme. The keynote papers addressed issues such as the gender aspects of draught animal power and of market-driven technology promotion, and presented gender-sensitive versions of participatory techniques such as Farming Systems Development and Participatory Rural Appraisal (PRA). In the working groups, these themes were further discussed and practised.

Most important, perhaps, was the last day, in which the participants were asked to make recommendations based on the following question: 'What should an organization like FAO or the AGROTEC project do to convince your colleagues of the importance of integrating gender in their work?' The formulation 'your colleagues' was chosen to separate the question from the participants and their self-image while still eliciting realistic information on how to approach engineers.

The list produced by the participants contained a number of concrete practical ideas, as well as recommendations regarding the approach or the style which should be taken when bringing gender issues to the attention of engineers. The latter are especially interesting: their overall message is quite clear and is probably well paraphrased in the first item on the list below: 'Whisper, don't shout,' It was clear from the workshop that male engineers, at least in southern and eastern African countries, are much more open to the gender message if a threatening and polarizing approach can be avoided.

Recommendations from the workshop participants: approaches to use when discussing gender with engineers

- Whisper, don't shout.
- Don't patronize.
- Don't use confrontational strategies: or begin with 'gender workshops' or statistics which put men on the defensive.
- Don't assume that traditional cultures are automatically negative.
- Gender-sensitization should be approached through participatory methods.
- Don't feminize the process: use women and men.
- Focus on the family and not just on women: illustrate that the gender approach and gender equality have economic and social benefits for the family as a whole.
- Recognize and respect cultural norms and existing bonds within the community.
- Gender policies should be developed within the organization rather than imposed from above.
- Persuade through personal experiences.
- Acknowledge people who are already making an effort to include gender in their work (give credit where it's due).

Interviews

To get a better idea of agricultural engineers' own thinking, perception and knowledge about gender and to get a clearer picture of what kind of information they would be willing to receive, twenty male and four female agricultural engineers from southern and eastern Africa were interviewed. The interviews were conducted by a male agricultural engineer and elicited some quite honest insights on the subject.

The answers depicted a range of attitudes. Some of the engineers just did not seem to see why women would be disadvantaged compared to men. Others had experience of gender training and had found the subject threatening and unpleasant. One quote from a Zambian senior engineer illustrates this: 'Yes, I attended training courses in which gender aspects were part of the course. In the past, these courses used to be not useful at all. There was a lot of fighting and accusing between the groups. For example women would give presentations with charts which showed that women work sixteen hours a day and men only five. The question is who is to blame for this.' Clearly, this engineer had the impressions that the presentation of such data was an implicit accusation of men in general and maybe even of himself in particular.

Other respondents again had a clear interest in the differences between men and women, but were rather inconsistent and confused about the need for taking these into account and the need for change. Frequently, engineers did not distinguish between just including women in their project work (i.e. setting targets for numbers of women included on the project teams and in the beneficiary groups), which can be fruitless as a way of bringing benefits to the majority of women in any community, and using whatever ways are necessary actively to reach and benefit women (for example, using journalists, probably male because there are few female journalists in many countries, to get issues raised in national and local media which are heard/read/watched by women beneficiaries).

Then there were some interviewed engineers whose interest in gender seemed strongly coloured by the hope of receiving funds by means of this magic word. Finally, some engineers were quite open-minded about needs and rights of women, and these may signal a new generation of male engineers.

All in all, it was concluded from the interviews that it is useful and possible to address engineers with material on gender, as long as they are approached as the informed and committed professionals that they generally are, and as long as the gender issues are presented in ways that address issues that the engineers find important. It is also possible to design and implement projects that are successful in improving farmers' lives; projects that reach not just a few farmers, but 'each and every farmer' who needs support.

Booklet: *Making Each and Every Farmer Count*

The third activity, building on the results of the workshop and the interviews, was the production of a booklet featuring six case studies on gender and agricultural engineering. The booklet is called *Making Each and Every Farmer Count: Participation in Agricultural Engineering Projects* (Lloyd-Laney 1998) and it is intended to sensitize those engineers who are not already convinced of the need to incorporate gender issues in project planning, but who are motivated to be effective in their work.

Approach   The people to whom the booklet is intended to appeal may not 'believe' in gender or participation (and they may find that they are made to feel guilty about that) because they have not yet been able to see how it helps them to get better results. The booklet tries to encourage them not just to look further at participatory techniques because gender experts say so, but because it is likely that by doing so they will have more successful projects.

In recognition of this and in line with the instrumental approach, the booklet avoids the use of the words 'gender' and 'participation' at first. Too often professionals have already heard these words and have formed their own opinions of what they mean. They may think 'gender' means simply to get more women involved, and 'partici-pation' means to get more people to come to meetings, and they may not see a use for either of these.

The booklet stresses the importance of the active engagement of farmers so that they will recognize how their investment in time and knowledge in the project is going to benefit them and their com-munities. This kind of engagement goes beyond participation. It implies that the commitment from the farmer is based on the benefit that the project has to herself or himself and not on willingness to please the project field worker. This basis for farmers' involvement is much more likely to lead to sustainability. The project staff does not have to convince its beneficiaries to continue with the new technology after the end of the project cycle; the farmers will already have worked that out for themselves before they even make the decision to come to the first meeting.

Thus, the booklet aims to help persuade the target audience not to flinch at the words 'gender' and 'participation' in future, but to listen to what people are saying about them and to find out for themselves if they provide clues for making their own projects better.

It is important to recognize the fact that gender awareness does not appear overnight but rather as a result of a series of steps which each person must take, starting with a recognition that the concept is an important and desirable one. Again, the booklet is meant to inspire the reader to take this first step.

Contents The booklet includes six practical examples of projects. Some have adopted a gender-aware approach in project planning and implementation and some have not. The booklet also includes an introduction and overview narrative of its purpose; a summary of the reasons why gender is an important issue in any development project; glossary of terms; bibliography; contacts and a pull-out poster featuring cartoons.

The six case studies describe the implementation and the resultant impacts of projects which have attempted to incorporate gender issues into their design, execution and evaluation, as well as of projects which made no attempt to incorporate these needs. The cases, for which the interviews described above were an important source, were chosen to cover the broad agricultural engineering sector; they are from five different Sub-Saharan African countries and from six different fields of agricultural engineering. They are the following:

- The Kebkabeiya Smallholder Project, the Sudan: *a plough for every household*
- Conservation Tillage Project, Zimbabwe: *water for life*
- On-farm storage structures for agricultural produce, Kenya: *the ventilated maize crib*

- Shea butter production, Ghana: *space to listen, in order to learn*
- Biogas digesters, Tanzania: *small is beautiful*
- The Mbeya Oxenization Project, Tanzania: *introducing animal traction*

Inside the booklet there is a pull-out poster, featuring cartoon strips that present stereotypical ways in which agricultural engineers can look at the different needs of men and women in their projects, and of how gender specialists interact with agricultural engineers. The cartoons use language and situations which are non-confrontational, in which the audience may recognize themselves, and understand that perhaps these are views and approaches which might need to be reassessed. Again, the point is not to show the agricultural engineers as 'the bad guys/girls' and the gender specialists as 'the good guys/girls', but to work *with* the engineers and practitioners in ways which will allow them to acknowledge that they perhaps have not been aware of the needs of different groups, or had the tools to respond to meeting these different needs.

Follow-up activities

If possible, AGSE is considering the production of a 'Partnership Presentation Package' as a supplement to the booklet, which would be made available to specialized presenters. It would include guidelines on how to present the package, a film slide series with accompanying scripts and a set of overheads. It could be helpful in achieving gender awareness among the target audience through presentations and discussions in university seminars, international conferences and regional workshops. Once this awareness is starting to become imbedded in the individual person, the next step would be to design more practical technical guidelines, or refer agricultural engineers to existing ones, to support them in addressing gender issues in an appropriate way in their day-to-day work.

8. Gender and transport

Priyanthi Fernando

This chapter highlights the main issues relating to gender and transport and examines how these issues have been integrated into strategies dealing with transport. The focus is on rural transport. It draws on the existing literature as well as on the author's experience with the rural transport programmes of Intermediate Technology in Sri Lanka and Kenya.

Conventional transport policies and planning and much development assistance have concentrated on building transport infrastructure, mainly roads. The development of roads implies an increased use of motorized vehicles. The seriousness of the environmental threat posed by increased motorization is highlighted and challenged by environmentalists and the sustainable transport movement in developed and developing countries.

There is, however, an alternative scenario that receives much less attention. Many of the villages in developing countries are not linked to road networks and, where they are, most villagers do not own or have no access to motorized transport. People in a majority of the villages of developing countries travel on foot, carrying their goods on their backs or on their heads. They travel considerable distances to collect water and firewood, to take goods to the markets, and to access education and health services. The time and energy that people must spend on these transport activities severely constrain their ability to pursue other livelihood-enhancing opportunities. The low productivity of rural transport tasks represents a waste of human energy. The alternative scenario that attempts to deal with these rural transport issues is the subject of this chapter.

Key issues in gender and rural transport

There are three key issues relating to gender and rural transport. These are: the unequal distribution of the transport burden, the unequal access to efficient transport technologies; and the invisibility of women's transport needs in transport planning.

Unequal distribution of the transport burden The key issue in gender and transport in rural areas in developing countries is the different amounts of time and energy that women and men spend in carrying out transport tasks. Gender differences in roles and responsibilities result in an unequal distribution of the transport burden. Studies in rural transport activities have, almost without exception, indicated that women spend more time in transport activities than men. The time spent in transport activities consumes a relatively high proportion of a woman's working day. This is in a context where women typically work twelve to thirteen hours more per week than men in Africa, Asia and the Pacific. One study in Mozambique found that women spend seven hours a day on transport activities: 3.4 hours per day transporting agricultural produce and materials and another 3.6 hours per day transporting firewood and water for the household (Hook 1994). Surveys in a number of African countries have shown that women account for about 65 per cent of all household time spent in transport activities and between 66 and 84 per cent of all energy (Doran 1996). In Makate in Tanzania, a typical woman spends about 1,650 hours per annum or over thirty hours every week on transport. In Ghana the time spent is 1,000 hours per annum or twenty hours per week. During harvesting and marketing seasons, these workloads are considerably greater (Dawson and Barwell 1993).

Much of women's transport burden is related to their reproductive or domestic responsibilities. Water and fuelwood collection accounts for 50 per cent of the time and effort spent on transport tasks. For many women this workload has increased during the last decades. Deforestation and overgrazing of pasture lands has led to soil erosion and to loss of fuel wood and depletion of water sources. This has increased the time and energy that women must devote to firewood and water collection. Extensification of cultivation and increased cash cropping have led to greater need for transport of inputs and produce. In the Himalayas, gathering fuelwood took no more than two hours in the foothills a generation ago. Today it takes a full day of trudging further up the mountains. In the Sudan, the time spent gathering fuelwood has increased fourfold in a decade. In Mozambique, women spend more than fifteen hours a day collecting water, and in Senegal about seventeen-and-a-half hours (UNDP 1995). Changing demographic and land-use patterns have made the distance to fields, water and firewood sources greater, increasing travel times to these sources. Increased use of educational and modern health facilities and women's engagement in wage labour and petty trading have also increased women's transport activities.

The imbalanced distribution of the transport burden restricts time and energy available for women for economic activities and family welfare. The heavy loads and energy required also take their toll on women's health and on the health of their infants. A study in Tanzania found positive correlation between women's heavy labour contributions and low birth weights of babies born during periods of peak labour. Low birth weights are a major cause of infant mortality in Tanzania (Bantje 1980). The loads that women carry make demands on their metabolism that are not met by nutritional intake in many developing country villages. It also puts an excessive strain on their skeleton, leading to spine deformities and the early onset of arthritic diseases (Page 1996). Girl children are often kept out of school so that they can assist with transport and other domestic tasks.

Access to efficient transport technologies The use of more efficient transport technologies can reduce the time and energy that women spend on transport tasks. The second issue in gender and transport relates to women's access to these means of transport.

In most developing countries, women have less access to assets and fewer rights to dispose of them. This restricts their ability to own and acquire appropriate time-saving transport technologies. Fewer women than men ride bicycles, use oxcarts or wheelbarrows or hire transport services (Doran 1996). In many African societies, donkeys are designated as animals to be used by women and they enable women to carry out their domestic transport activities more efficiently. Even then, in many of these societies, it is the men who own and control the animals and women are unable to purchase or sell donkeys (Fernando 1997). Social attitudes and beliefs also restrict women's access to means of transport. Cycling is a very common form of transport in many Asian and some African societies but women's use of bicycles is limited to pillion passenger or passenger in a cycle rickshaw. Women do not usually have the purchasing power to acquire a bicycle nor in many cases is there social acceptance of women riding one. A project for introducing bicycle trailers to rural communities in Sri Lanka by Intermediate Technology found that many women simply did not cycle. The trailers were being bought by men and used for productive and income-generating activities. Only 58 per cent of the trailers were being used for collecting water and 33 per cent for collecting firewood (Doran 1996). Similarly, in the Mbale District of Uganda, bicycle ownership and use was monopolized by men (Malmberg 1994a). Both in Sri Lanka and Uganda some of the transport burden of the women was transferred to men, through husbands or sons using the bicycle trailer to fetch water. Among the tribal Santhal of Bihar too, increased use of bicycles by the men folk resulted in a reduction of the women's transport burden as the men began taking forest products to the market. However, this also led to women losing control over the sale of the forest produce that they collected and prepared (Rao ongoing).

Traditional beliefs about what women should or should not do militate against women's use of transport technologies. For instance, in many traditional societies women are not expected to work with large livestock. This precludes their access to animal carts for transport. In Zimbabwe they are rarely seen driving ox-drawn scotch carts. One reason is that they are regarded as incapable of managing work animals. Yet owing to extensive male migration, women often perform 'male' tasks with teams of oxen and steel ploughs (IT Transport Ltd 1996).

In short, gender power relations can inhibit the adoption of transport technologies by women. Men have cash incomes and access to income-generating activities that enable them to control the acquisition and use of the technology. It is also a consequence of complex cultural factors that generate negative perceptions of, for instance, women riding bicycles.

In Africa, the perception of women and girls as a major transport form, head-loading goods for their households as well as for purchasers of their services, has inhibited the development of transport devices that could be used to take the load off the head at low cost (Jeff Turner, personal communication). Bryceson and Howe state that African women frequently express the view that a man, having paid the bride price, then expects his wife to perform load-carrying duties as part of her obligations to her husband's household (Bryceson and Howe 1993). Men, who are the decision-makers in most households, will invest in reducing women's transport burden only if there is a direct benefit to themselves. In Tanzania, the men supported an improved water supply scheme only because their meals were delayed because women spent so much time fetching water (Doran 1996). In the Kitui region of Kenya, water sources were so distant that men often had to help the women with carrying the water. Curtis (1986) considers this one of the reasons for the high ownership of donkeys among the households in the area.

As is the case for many other technologies, women's access to transport technologies is also constrained by the inappropriateness of the design of the technology and its method of dissemination. The Makate Integrated Rural Transport Project in Tanzania promoted donkeys and wheelbarrows as appropriate transport technologies to address the rural transport burden of village communities. Their use by women was limited. The panniers that were being used for the donkeys were inappropriately designed for carrying firewood. Loading donkeys required two people. Since women (particularly in women-headed households) worked alone, this was a problem. The project's promotional messages also did not reach a large number of women. Because of their restricted mobility women had only limited exposure to donkey use where the animals were being used in neighbouring villages or by traders. Nor was there much evidence of women using the wheelbarrows in Makate. This was because the predominant perception was that the wheelbarrows could only be used for construction work because the majority were used by men to carry bricks and sand. Women also found that using both hands to push a wheelbarrow could be a disadvantage when carrying or walking with children (Jennings 1992).

Invisibility of women in transport planning The third issue in gender and transport is the invisibility of women to most transport professionals. Transport planning for rural areas of developing countries has traditionally been concerned with economic sectors –

mainly with the transport of primary produce to cities and the distribution of manufactured goods to the periphery. This orientation has been challenged by planners who have been dissatisfied with the conventional system and become increasingly concerned with unemployment and poverty issues. The challenge has led to the development of alternative planning methodologies.

Initially the alternative focused on household demand for rural travel and transport identified through surveys using the household as a unit of analysis. This approach was described as Integrated Rural Transport Planning (IRTP) and was used in Tanzania and Malawi. It was next tried out in the Philippines and renamed Integrated Rural Accessibility Planning (IRAP) to reflect the emphasis on accessibility of rural households to essential facilities and services. The difference between transport planning and accessibility planning is that the former focuses on ways to improve mobility through improved infrastructure and provision of transport services. The latter recognizes that transport problems can be solved in two complementary ways: one is to increase mobility through an improved transport system, the other is to locate facilities and services closer to people. The IRAP process uses a participatory methodology involving communities (or their representatives) to identify the full range of rural travel and transport demands, that is, the access to domestic, economic and social needs. It is being used as a planning tool in the decentralized administration of the Philippines, where it not only provides transport solutions but also provides a general framework for the production of development plans. IRAP has also been introduced in several other countries such as Bangladesh, Malawi and Laos.

The IRTP methodology and the IRAP process (and the studies that preceded their development) were able to identify the disproportionate transport burden undertaken by women and the dominance of subsistence tasks over tasks for market production. Interventions that provide solutions to these problems, however, have been limited. The limitation could result from the low participation of women in the decision-making processes that prioritize and design the interventions. It is also related to the reluctance of planners and decision-makers to move away from purely economic criteria to those that value the social benefits of interventions.

In the Makate District of Tanzania, where pioneering work on integrated rural transport planning and intervention took place, the introduction of donkeys and wheelbarrows had, as we saw above, limited impact on easing women's transport burden. Partly this was due to the way the technology was designed and disseminated. The economic orientation of transport interventions also led to an emphasis on the purchase of donkeys, rather than on systems for hiring them. In a situation where women had little disposable income, the scheme to purchase donkeys reinforced gender inequalities in access and control of resources and limited the potential benefit to women. In a village with eighty-two donkey-owning households, the donkeys (owned by male heads of households) were used to carry home the harvest but were not used to carry water or firewood.

The Makate project also prioritized the improvement of paths and tracks as a way of tackling the transport problem. The self-help interventions that were required to improve the quality of the paths and tracks, however, put considerable pressure on the women. Contributing their labour left them with less time for their agricultural activities. They predicted lower harvests and greater food insecurity as a result (Jennings 1992).

The IRAP methodology also provides planners with the information that can enable the prioritization of interventions that bring facilities and services closer to people. The evidence of the impact of such interventions on women's transport burden is scarce. Well-designed rural water projects that provide a reliable all-year-round supply of potable water closer to home than the natural source, and well-designed wood lot schemes, can reduce the time and energy that women spend on water and firewood collection. The introduction of improved wood-burning stoves can reduce firewood consumption with an equivalent reduction in the time and energy spent on collection. The provision of grinding mills closer to the home can reduce the transport burden when households are using a more distant mill. (If grinding mills are replacing traditional home-based processing, then there is an increase in the transport task, but a reduction in the overall burden of the activity.) A study of villages with and without piped water in Makate indicated that households saved approximately 300 hours annually with a piped water scheme, and that 80 per cent of this time was saved by women. In Makate, functioning grinding mills reduced the tonne/km load by more than 90 per cent, the time by nearly 80 per cent. Ninety per cent of this benefit accrued to women (Sieber 1996). On the other hand, Malmberg Calvo's examination of several similar interventions shows that many have had a limited impact on the transport burden of rural women. This has been the case particularly where the improved source of water is no more accessible than the traditional source, where wood lots have focused on the production of timber for commercial rather than domestic use and where the 'improved' stoves are inappropriate to the local food preparation culture. This is largely due to the lack of involvement of women in their design and implementation (Malmberg 1994b). It is also likely that these interventions will be considered 'social' and not receive priority in development plans.

Towards an integration of gender and rural transport

Integrating gender into rural transport interventions The successful integration of gender into rural transport interventions has been constrained by two factors: the lack of participation of women both in the planning process and in the design of the interventions, and the economic argument that continues to dominate planning.

There is some evidence emerging from micro-level strategies that points to the fact that village people (if not planners) do value the social benefits from improved transport technologies and are willing to invest in their acquisition. This is particularly true if the production and dissemination of these technologies are supported by innovative credit arrangements and participatory technology development.

The Rural Transport Programme of Intermediate Technology, Kenya (IT Kenya) provides several examples. In Kathekani, IT Kenya is working with local district committees to promote the use of carts. The local committee implements a credit scheme that provides families in the area with the opportunity to purchase carts manufactured by local *fundi* (artisans). The carts have been purchased by a number of families in the area and are used mainly for subsistence (rather than market-oriented) tasks. They are owned usually by the male heads of households. The carts are being used for water collection, for firewood collection, for carrying manure to the *shambas* (fields) and for transporting harvest from the fields to the homestead. In a largely subsistence-based village economy, the use of this intermediate means of transport has greatly reduced the time and energy women spend on transport tasks.

IT Kenya has also been promoting the increased use of donkeys by Maasai women in the Kajiado District for fetching and carrying firewood and water. Traditionally, the Maasai have used donkeys for the transport of household goods in their transhumance activities. The use of donkeys for firewood and water collection was limited (at least in the Kajiado District). IT Kenya's interventions encouraged greater use of donkeys. The project adopted a participatory approach. It worked with Maasai women to develop appropriate panniers and sought to overcome traditional beliefs about the use of donkeys through visits of both Maasai women and men to areas where donkeys were being extensively used. In a recent review of the project, a comparison of two Maasai women indicated that the woman using a donkey to carry water was able to reduce the time spent on water collection by as many as twenty-five hours per week. The women saw this time saved as valuable for carrying out other tasks, for rest and leisure and for more involvement in community work (Fernando and Keter 1996).

In Western Kenya, IT Kenya works with a local NGO, Future Forest, to promote the use of donkeys by women's groups. The project adapted an existing 'merry-go-round' savings and credit scheme to enable a women's group to purchase donkeys. Eighteen members of the group divided themselves into smaller groups of three. When each of the smaller groups had saved half of the cost of the donkey, Future Forest provided the balance on credit, and the women purchased a donkey. Three women collectively own a donkey and use it for collecting water and for other transport tasks. The frequency of trips has not changed, but the women benefit from a reduction in the burden of head loading and from the ability to collect twice as much water with less effort (Fernando and Keter 1996).

Integrating access and mobility issues into gender strategies While it is important that gender issues are integrated into rural transport strategies, it is also important that strategies addressing women's empowerment address access and mobility issues. Lack of access and mobility leads to isolation and isolation is poverty. It inhibits the poor from taking advantage of employment and income-generating opportunities, it limits access to education and health services and even to new ideas and innovations.

For women farmers and traders in Africa and Asia, lack of appropriate transport technologies and services for transporting their produce limits their marketing opportunities and reduces their potential incomes. For farmers this means being forced to sell their harvest to middlemen at low prices. In Ahmedabad, India, women vegetable vendors are not allowed to travel by city transport bus with their produce, forcing them either to walk or to pay half a day's earnings for scooter hire (Bhatt 1989). An ongoing study in Burkina Faso will show how lack of access to transport technologies inhibits women garbage collectors in Ouagadougou from expanding their business (Damiba ongoing). Conversely, women's capacity to make use of opportunities for income-generation can be constrained by the toll that transport tasks take on their time and energy. The Self-Employed Women's Association (SEWA), working with women in the dry regions of Gujarat, has seen that the women are able to take advantage of its loan scheme and technical assistance because a water supply scheme reduced the time they spent on water collection.

Increased mobility can also change gender power relations. One of the most dramatic examples comes from Pudukottai District in Tamil Nadu in South India. A project aimed at total literacy included women's mobility as a key element of the literacy campaign and encouraged women in the area to learn to ride bicycles. The project also implemented a credit scheme that facilitated women's access to bicycles. About one-fourth of all the women in the district learned to ride bicycles. Among the women are agricultural workers, quarry labourers, village health nurses, traditional craftswomen and rural schoolteachers. Cycling has helped women selling agricultural and other produce to cut down on time wasted in waiting for buses, transporting water and fetching children from school. It also has given them a sense of freedom and confidence and increased their status within the society (Rao 1993; Sainath 1995).

Future directions Integrating gender issues into rural transport strategies requires two complementary approaches. First, it requires ways of identifying the differences in transport needs and priorities. Approaches to transport planning such as IRAP provide the framework through which such differences can be identified, provided that

the participatory methodology has no social biases and con-
scientiously includes representation of both genders.

Second, it requires ways in which unequal access to resources and
to the benefits of transport (and other) interventions can be addressed.
The micro-level experience indicates this includes strategies that
involve the participation of women, that work closely with local
organizations, that target women taking into account their social,
economic and cultural realities and that involve innovative credit
arrangements. These approaches are, however, far from mainstream.
Much rural transport activity continues to ignore the gender differences in needs. There are several areas in which more work needs
to be done.

Better identification of the problem   There is a need for better
gender-disaggregated data and research to provide more information
on rural transport problems, needs and priorities. The extent of
women's transport burden in Africa has been well documented. There
is, however, limited knowledge of the types of problems faced by
women in Asia, where the social, economic, cultural and geographical
context is very different. Large densities of population, the greater
prevalence of a wide range of intermediate means of transport, the
lower visibility of women head loading or back carrying and the
cultural restrictions to women's mobility, has led to the assumption
that there is less inequality in the distribution of transport tasks.
This needs to be verified.

More interventions   Many of the interventions for addressing
women's transport burden have focused on the introduction of means
of transport (donkeys, bicycles and trailers). We have some evidence
(though not enough) on how these interventions can be appropriately
designed and disseminated to address inherent gender inequalities.
We have much less information on the other dimensions of rural
transport strategies: the provision of local transport infrastructure,
the expansion of rural transport services and the provision of facilities
and services closer to the people.

Greater understanding of impact   There is little evidence of the
impact that transport and 'non-transport' interventions (i.e. interventions that bring facilities and services closer to people) have on

women's transport burden. The lack of information on the impact of the provision of facilities and services closer to people is not a result of the lack of such interventions. Improved water supply schemes, wood lots, provision of grain mills or health centres or schools are implemented within the broader framework of rural development. The compartmentalization of these rural infrastructure projects from rural transport issues has precluded the analysis of their benefits from a transport needs perspective.

The field of rural transport intervention is, as pointed out in this chapter, fairly recent. Many of the micro-level projects described here are new. This means that the impact of transport interventions on the gender inequalities of access to transport resources and benefits is also limited. It is important that there is a continuous monitoring of the potential impact of these interventions on women and men.

Increased women's participation The most critical issue that still has to be addressed is the need for an expanded role for women in decision-making about transport policies, priorities and investments at the national level, at the level of decentralized administration where much rural transport planning will take place in the future, and within communities. Without such participation it is difficult to see how rural transport strategies can include gender issues in ways that can have practical implications for the lives of women.

Conclusions

Rural transport issues have only recently received the attention of transport planners and technologists. Studies in rural transport have indicated that there is gender inequality in the transport burden and in the types of interventions designed to alleviate the burden. Women spend more time and energy than men on transport tasks and have less access to the technologies that help reduce this effort. As a result, there is a considerable waste of human energy on what is, essentially, low productive activity. The non-economic nature of the bulk of women's transport tasks and the low participation of women in the decision-making processes that prioritize and design inter-ventions have constrained the implementation of more appropriate strategies. There is, however, some encouraging evidence of practical examples of innovative projects that have had a positive impact on women. Much more needs to be done in terms of documenting the problem, providing case studies of good practice and of measuring impact.

9. Gender and urban waste management

Maria S. Muller

Citizens in many cities of the world are increasingly concerned about the amounts of garbage lying uncollected in the streets, causing inconvenience, environmental pollution and serious health risks. Although government authorities apply all the means at their disposal, the piles of wastes only seem to grow from day to day. These concerns have resulted in increasing attention being paid to urban waste management and new waste management technologies. Strategies are being developed to enlist the private formal sector in the ongoing effort to collect, transport, treat, recycle and dispose of waste. Also neighbourhood communities, associations and small, informal enterprises are encouraged to collect and/or transform household wastes with the explicit aim of creating employment and keeping their own living environment clean and healthy.

This chapter shows that it is both appropriate and necessary to apply a gender perspective to waste management, since waste management affects the lives of both men and women, though not in the same way, and both men and women participate, in different ways, in waste activities. Indeed, the definition of waste itself is 'gendered'. The challenge in waste management is to specify what a gender perspective means in concrete terms in the daily practice of waste activities, and to develop strategies of waste management that decrease rather than increase inequalities between men and women.

This chapter is based on a series of about forty case studies from Asia, Latin America and Africa, carried out between 1995 and 1998 under the Urban Waste Expertise Programme (UWEP). The UWEP, a six-year programme financed by the Netherlands Development Agency and co-ordinated by the Dutch NGO WASTE, was set up to document the existing waste practices of people, community organizations and informal enterprises in low-income urban neighbourhoods, and to support new initiatives in this field. Although these case studies concern a variety of waste activities, they do show general patterns regarding the involvement of women and men in these activities.

Complexities of waste management Waste management in cities is a complex affair: many different materials, activities and organizations are involved. Waste management deals with a diverse set of waste materials, including household garbage, human excreta, waste water, and so on. It also concerns a range of activities, including:

- collecting human and solid wastes
- buying and selling of household garbage
- reusing waste materials (recycling waste)
- disposing of human and solid wastes in a safe manner
- street cleaning

Decisions regarding these activities are taken on several levels, by individuals, households, community committees, enterprises and government authorities. Waste management technologies are in greater or lesser degree part of most of these activities. But waste management is concerned with institutional linkages among organizations as much as with technology; it concerns environmental and economic consequences, as well as having social implications. Add to this a gender dimension and we have a challenging field for urban development strategies, a field that is not yet well known.

The conventional technology for waste collection, treatment and disposal is large and capital-intensive, and relies on advanced technical expertise. Imported from Western countries, this technology is not wholly adequate to serve the needs of Third World cities. With technically advanced conventional equipment the municipal authorities can collect only a small proportion of the waste produced daily, concentrating on the most accessible, wealthier residential areas, the business centre and some others. Low- and middle-income areas are hardly served when only conventional equipment is used.

The breakdown of conventional waste management in these lower-income areas shows that it is necessary to reconsider the various elements in waste management. At present people and organizations are engaged in developing new types of waste collection services, new technologies for the reuse of waste materials, new forms of institutional organization, new policies, new forms of influence and co-ordination. A new 'practical wisdom' in waste management is in the making through experiments and pilot projects. Neighbourhoods and cities are trying to reorganize themselves in order better to serve the interests of their residents in the waste sector. At this time it is necessary to ensure that the interests of women are also recognized.

Gender In waste management as elsewhere, the introduction of a gender perspective implies a focus on the social relations between men and women (which is more than just looking at the category 'women'). The final objective of integrating a gender perspective is to reduce the inequality of women and men in society. It is necessary to apply knowledge on the all-persuasive effects of gender to a new sector: urban waste management. As in other sectors – for example provision of water supply, housing improvement – the implications of gender must be 'translated' in terms of actual operations of the specific sector.

Such translated information may assist environmental NGOs to understand the social and gender implications of their work, and assist gender and development NGOs to apply their ideas to waste issues in urban communities. At present the NGOs, local authorities and professionals in these two broad fields find it difficult to understand each other, because the cross-cutting concerns of gender and waste management have not been elaborated. Few studies exist to date. However, it is clear that gender aspects are relevant in waste management. Basically they can be discerned on three levels: gender aspects related to waste as a source of income, gender aspects related to waste as a health and environment hazard, and gender aspects of defining community needs and promoting community participation.

Gender aspects of waste as a source of income

Waste handling is an important source of income, especially for poorer women (Huysman 1994). Women's involvement in waste handling as an income-generating activity is characterized by a number of gender-specific characteristics. In comparison to men, women are mainly engaged in activities requiring less education, fewer skills and a smaller range of physical mobility. Thus, women are often involved in waste picking from dump sites and in sorting and washing waste, but very seldom work with waste-processing machines. Likewise, they are often involved in waste collection, but less often in waste transportation.

Women involved in waste activities generally earn less than men. Several forces seem to be at work here. First, since waste handling offers great income opportunities, the field is subject to the prevailing forces of competition and of inequality in a society. Generally such forces reinforce existing inequalities. Women are also more vulnerable to exploitation by waste dealers and employers. Moreover, they do not have the range of social-cum-business contacts over a wide area of the city, which men often have, that give access to personal credit and favourable market opportunities.

In general, micro-enterprises in the waste sector seem to be more often initiated, operated and managed by men. There are, however, examples of all-women's enterprises or co-operatives. Interestingly, when the initiative for a waste-related enterprise is taken by a group of women, they tend to co-opt or employ other women (Lapid et al. 1998). The same happens when groups are formed for the purpose of acquiring and managing micro-loans. Likewise, men's enterprises in this sector mainly employ other men.

Cultural barriers When engaged as waste collection labourers, women are reliable workers. As income opportunities for illiterate women are scarce, they are prepared to overcome the barriers of distance and of culture. For example, they will walk four hours to and from work at the neighbourhood designated for waste collection (Burkina Faso) or work in the male world of the harbour (Pakistan) (Shamsi and Ahmed 1998). These women transgress social rules that limit women's mobility to the immediate neighbourhood, because of the high priority of gaining a living for themselves and their dependants.

Women as waste workers face cultural barriers in several ways. Both men and women face the disrespect of fellow-citizens, as handling untreated waste materials is considered demeaning. In addition, women who are cleaning public places such as streets or bus stations are often insulted or harassed (India). Working in remote sites such as waste dumps or factory sites, they may be assaulted. And if women who earn their own income with garbage collection also assert themselves in the family (for example by claiming the right to spend their money as they see fit), they may find themselves the centre of social conflict. There is an interesting case (Burkina Faso) where the NGO managed to show women how to become more 'polite' in their assertiveness (UWEP 1998).

Employment and subcontracting policies Employment policies may have a negative effect on women. It can be in the interest of overall urban waste management to integrate informal sector services into the formal sector through direct employment of waste labourers, or through subcontracting to small enterprises. For example, in some cities women form the majority of workers in informal services to collect human excreta. But when a municipal department decides (as in Ghaziabad, India) to place the excreta collection workers on the municipal payroll, it may turn out that 70 per cent of these employees are men (UWEP 1998).

Similar mechanisms may be in operation when small enterprises obtain municipal subcontracts in the waste sector. Often such contracts go to male-owned enterprises, offering them relative stability of income. Women's formal and informal waste activities will usually experience an intensified competition from these enterprises.

Waste technologies When new technologies are introduced for waste collection, disposal or recycling, gender aspects will again play a role. A series of questions arise that need to be considered. For example, can women-owned enterprises as well as men-owned enterprises afford the higher investment? Are women-owned enterprises able to generate the higher work volume needed to pay for this investment, to the same extent that men-owned or mixed enterprises can? Do women too have the managerial expertise required for a greater volume of work? Do women have an equal chance to get the necessary training? Can women as well as men continue with related income-earning activities, such as sorting the waste? How does the new technology affect the health of women and that of men? Does it create equal risks or offer equal protection against health risks? Is the technology adequate for women? In one case in Dakar, Senegal, where a women's enterprise had gained a formal subcontract, the municipality had provided hand-carts and shovels. The women complained that the hand-carts were too unwieldy and too heavy and they suffered from backaches and injuries because of the equipment (UWEP 1998). It is not known whether the men in other micro-enterprises had the same complaints as the women.

Leaving such gender issues to the existing forces of competition and inequality in a society will surely lead to a growing socio-economic disadvantage for women. That is the lesson from the introduction of technology to small enterprises in other parts of economic life. Here lies a task for NGOs and committed professionals, to design gender-specific programmes supporting the introduction of new waste technologies.

Gender aspects of waste as an environmental and health risk

Women, with their domestic and caring tasks, have an obvious interest in an immediate living environment that enables them to carry out their tasks easily. Taking household garbage to street corner dustbins may be easy, but it is not so easy when the distance between house and dustbin is too large. It is natural that children fall ill, but it demands unnecessary effort when children frequently become ill due to vermin roaming in piles of uncollected garbage.

Environmental monitoring   Waste management is more than the provision of services; it also involves behaviour of people who carry out waste-related activities. This behaviour can be influenced. Experiences show that, given the opportunity and rising to the occasion, women are the most effective residents in monitoring environmental cleanliness. They can do this by walking regular rounds in the immediate neighbourhood to check whether the waste collection services have done their work well and properly (Pakistan, the Philippines) (UWEP 1998). Women, as immediate neighbours, may also encourage each other to maintain cleanliness around the house and in the street, or to pay for waste collection. They may begin to see this as a shared concern through participation in a programme of dialogue-oriented environmental health education (Burkina Faso).

Health Gender-specific health risks of working with waste materials
are not yet documented, but can be deduced. Data are available
showing that people who have physical contact with human excreta
or other raw waste materials contract diseases like hepatitis and
diarrhoea and suffer from skin infections more frequently than people
not so employed. It depends on the gender division of labour whether
men or women are more exposed to such health risks and how this
affects the workers' children.

Gender aspects of defining needs and decision-making

Public gatherings and committee meetings are often the means of
consulting the community about people's wishes. Regarding the
gender aspects of participation in such gatherings, it is observed
everywhere that women are most active on street-level committees.
They also participate in the next highest level of meetings, the
neighbourhood meetings, sometimes even as leaders, but this is less
frequent.

Several elements are at play when a community is consulted about
waste services. The first is that women and men are likely to have
different interests regarding environmental improvement, based on
the different use they make of the immediate environment. The
second is the nature of the consultation process itself, among others
the composition of the committee that takes decisions, and the forms
of representation between the lower- and the higher-level committees.

In one community-based project initiated by the municipality in
Goa, India, the 'community' was given the opportunity to make a
choice between two types of waste collection services, either a public
garbage container at street corners where residents could bring their
garbage at a low price; or waste collection from door to door at a
higher price. The community preferred the latter. No information is
available on the considerations leading up to this preference and
whether they differed between different social groups. Yet in this
case the views of men and women within a household are likely to
differ, depending, among other things, on which household member
is responsible for taking out the garbage, and which member of the
household is able and willing to pay for the collection service.

In another community in Kampala, Uganda, where undrained

storm water caused great problems, the highest neighbourhood committee was given the choice between two types of drainage system: a
sophisticated one, which would take three years before becoming
operational, or a simple one, to be operational before the next rainy
season. The neighbourhood committee chose the sophisticated one,
while the women, who were not represented on this level, would
have preferred the one which would alleviate their environmental
problems immediately (personal communication from Betty Kwagala,
Makerere Institute of Social Research, Kampala, Uganda).

In a third case, in Bamako, Mali, it was reported that women had
in the past been members of the highest neighbourhood waste
management committee, but had stopped participation all at once
'because they were too busy with earning money for their children to
waste time on meetings' (personal communication from CPAC,
Bamako, Mali). One would like to know the details of the history
that led up to this move.

It was observed in several cities that women-only meetings take
longer than mixed meetings or those with men only. One explanation
offered by NGO staff is that women take meetings as a social
opportunity to talk about the family and their children, their domestic
problems. As another explanation it was suggested that women continue a discussion until a high degree of consensus is reached, while
men would have a different style of meeting.

An important question about community consultation is the degree
to which it can contribute to a process of empowerment within the
community groups. Do men and women, and members of other
social groups, get equal chances to understand the issues involved
and to express their opinions? Simple but crucial factors that can
influence equal opportunities in this respect are, for example, the
choice of meeting place and meeting time, the language used, and
the division of representative tasks such as debating with the local
authorities. It is the task of support organizations to ensure that the
different participants do get equal chances.

A gendered definition of waste

The word 'waste' refers to something that is 'no longer serving a
purpose', something 'without value' (*Concise Oxford Dictionary*). Ob-
viously, however, some people consider waste materials as an income-

generating resource for their enterprise. They make compost out of organic waste, or are specialized in manufacturing new products from used rubber, glass, batteries, bones, etc. Seen from the point of view of women's domestic role, so-called waste materials could also be used as a resource within households. For example, oily milk packages may be used as fuel, or leftover food may be fed to pigs and goats. These resources do not contribute to an income, but do save on household expenditure. Thus, men and women may revalue waste materials for different purposes: 'waste' may be a domestic utility, a way of saving on expenditure, a means of earning money, or have some other meaning. In short, the definition of waste is gendered, and so is the definition of resource. This should be reflected when discussing waste management priorities during the community consultation process.

The following are some key questions that can be asked to find out the gendered definition of waste and resources. These are based on the questions formulated for the field of gender and the rural environment (Guijt 1994):

• What natural and social resources are important in local livelihoods?
• Who uses which resources?
• Who controls decisions about how resources are used?
• Who is helping to sustain local resources and who benefits from this?
• How is the situation changing?

In urban neighbourhoods, there are natural resources (such as domestic animals, trees and plants/vegetables), environmental resources (various types of waste materials, waste water, unbuilt space), and social resources (such as traditional and modern knowledge, skills, networks of social relationships, and channels of communication). Also, infrastructural facilities for drainage, sanitation and waste disposal are resources whose availability and maintenance influence women's and men's daily lives.

Answers to these questions about resources must be sought through a participatory process of research and consultation to ensure that men and women, boys and girls contribute and benefit in the best possible ways.

The vicious circle of inequality

Women (like other disadvantaged social groups, which may be defined on the basis of their age, caste, education, etc.) are in a disadvantaged position, in the sense of not being able to benefit from development opportunities, or even by getting into deeper poverty because of a development project. Opportunities for social advancement through new technology for waste recycling may come only to those people who are in a favourable position, through, for example, belonging to the 'right' social group, or living in the 'right' part of town. The factors that reinforce the disadvantaged position of women and other disadvantaged groups include:

- the play of prevailing forces of competition and inequality
- being left outside the consultation and decision-making process in the community
- having no access to the capital required for new technology
- having no access to information and training
- living in inaccessible places

Thus, disadvantaged groups may be caught in a vicious circle which can either be deepened or broken by outside intervention. Project strategies can affect this circle. UWEP case studies (UWEP 1997; 1998 [Burkina Faso]; see also Macdonald 1994, Holzner 1996) show that NGOs are able to support the development of an enterprise and at the same time ensure that women have chances equal to those of men to participate in that improved enterprise. Similarly, the process of information, consultation and planning of waste activities can be organized in such a way that women and social minorities can also take part. A variety of strategies may have to be applied concurrently. The case studies also show that NGOs that address gender inequalities usually have committed female staff members, whom they support with appropriate means and strategies. The committed female staff themselves have contacts with the national and international women's movement.

Conclusions and recommendations

The implications of gender in waste management are not well known. Using lessons drawn from general issues in gender and technology, micro-enterprise development, environment and rural development, and urban neighbourhood improvement, however, it can be recommended that:

- a gender perspective should be integrated in assessment studies, planning, implementation and monitoring of waste management projects; this should include a gender-specific analysis of how available waste and resources are valued and used
- the staff of support and development organizations should be made more aware of possible gender implications, among others by means of training programmes
- such training programmes should incorporate country-specific conditions

New technology has an effect on the chain of waste management activities beyond the specific activity for which the equipment is designed. Technology is also of social and economic importance to women, men, and their households. Therefore:

- organizations and experts should take the design of new equipment as the beginning of a process of consultation with the 'community' (men and women) and owners/workers of small enterprises; this should lead to flexible implementation
- technical training may have to use a combination of approaches in order to reach both women and men

It has been observed that support organizations such as NGOs or local authorities can be very influential in achieving a definite place for women as well as for men as active participants in enterprises or in development projects. Therefore:

- the (female) staff of support organizations should be enabled to strengthen their gender commitment through national and international contacts, project experience and training
- gender consciousness and commitment to the promotion of gender equality in waste management should be an important criterion in choosing partner organizations and local experts

Agencies that want to work towards a system of waste management which contributes to the reduction of social inequalities should:

- identify the different groups in the target population, and analyse the basic factors that maintain the position of disadvantaged groups such as women

- determine how these basic factors can be addressed to enable disadvantaged social groups also to benefit from new opportunities through waste management
- prepare project approaches that address these basic factors in combination with specific waste management requirements

Appendix

Factors to consider when introducing technology to women's enterprises

The list of twenty-three factors

A. Assessing the need

1. Good analysis of problems and their causes. (Is there really a problem that corresponds to this solution?)
2. Involvement of women and men.

. . . .

B. A business approach

3. Market situation.
4. Supply situation.
5. Calculating pay-back time of investment.
6. Business training.

. . . .

C. Necessary provisions

7. Organizing the production.
8. Credit provision.
9. Land and location.

. . . .

D. What is the best technical option?

10. Size of technical step.
11. Requirements for operation.
12. Technical soundness and durability.
13. Repair facilities and spare parts.
14. Training on operation, maintenance and repair.

. . . .

E.   (Un)intended effects

15.   Effects of the technology on the mechanized activity.
16.   Effects of the technology on linked activities.
17.   Effects on time and workload of women.
18.   Effects on the products and by-products.
19.   The issue of control.
. . . .

F.   The wider context

20.   Social-cultural constraints.
21.   Economic macro-environment.
22.   Political environment.
23.   Backward and forward linkages.
. . . .

Examples from the training participants

At the end of the training 'Introducing Technology to Women's Enterprises', which was held in November 1995 in Ho, Ghana, each participant was assigned one of the factors and asked to give an example from his or her own experience. Eleven participants wrote their story down.

Factor 3: Market situation An entrepreneur must know a lot about the market and marketing. He or she must also consider the five Ps of marketing. For example, research has to be done on what might be the best location for selling (P for Place), on how to attract customers (P for Promotion) and how to deal with competitors.

Stone quarry A project was started to put up a stone quarry. The raw materials, which are the stone and the hammer, were available. The stone is in fact free of charge, so when the women decided to crack the stone, there was no problem. But unfortunately in this project they did not make any effort to look for who would buy the stone, although a lot of people were putting up a house and thus probably would have been interested. Secondly, the women did not look at the competition. Most women in the village crack stone as their daily job. Usually the stone is parked along the road, so when the constructors come they buy the stone by the roadside. But these women were parking their stone in a valley and not near the road.

So the stone lay there for ages. Because they couldn't sell, the women were no longer motivated, refused to come to work and in the long run the project collapsed.

Factor 6: Business training Did the business members have a business training? Do they know about the complexity of mechanization, of its risks?

Gari processing After a feasibility study was carried out, the Regional Credit Union Officer held a training for the Sokode-Gbogame Women Group in business skills, including accounting, pricing and marketing. After this successful training, the women were introduced to *susu* (which is a traditional saving system) to begin with the Credit Union. There was a larger group of forty-two women. This group was divided into smaller groups of five persons each. The women were allowed to practice *susu* in turns of six months. Because they were successful, a working capital in the form of a loan, an amount of one million with an interest rate of 18%, was given to the women. With constant visits and supervision, the loans were paid back. This gave me confidence to introduce a cassava-grater machine to the group. Now they are producing gari about 50 kg every four weeks.

Factor 7: Organizing the production Should the enterprise be a group enterprise or an individual enterprise? Who takes the organizing role? Who actually runs the machine?

Cassava dough producing There is a small village in the Kpando District called Kudi Kofe. The inhabitants of that village are cassava dough producers. So I went to them and we discussed the best way they could increase their production. Fortunately, a man from the village abroad grouped some friends around and they donated a mill to the villagers for their work. Unfortunately, none of the group members knew how to operate the machine. So they had to employ a local miller. This local miller became rich, due to the fact that he was cheating them. So the group members were not able to pay back the machine, because they did not earn enough money. This situation brought about a quarrel in the group. The Queen Mother of the village resolved the problem by locking the door on the machine.

I feel that if there were proper organizations and trained personnel among the group, this would not have gone like this.

Factor 9: Land and location It is important to know whether the project site is not too far from the participants' living space.

Cassava grating machine A grater was given to the Kechiebi women group on a loan basis, to increase the women's gari processing group activities. The site for the installation of the machine was far at the outskirts of town. The project went on with individual women grating their raw cassava. Another individual, seeing this, bought a grater and installed it in the centre of the town. People were reluctant to carry their raw cassava to the project site, and preferred grating at the centrally located grating machine. The project market fell and there was confusion between leaders and project members. The group collapsed and the few members left took up cassava production which enabled them to pay back the cost of the machine and the interest.

Factor 11: Requirements for operation How stable is the supply? What are the costs and how stable are these?

Cassava grating machine The two main requirements for this project were cassava and fuel. The project was done by the women of Kpassa in the Nkwanta district.

When the project was started, a feasibility study was done by a donor agency who after that gave them a cassava grater as a loan of one million cedis. This loan had to be paid back in three years with an interest of 10 per cent. Before the work started, the women had a training without any charge from a private grater operator.

The work started on a very sound ground for six months. But when the rains set in, the women were having difficulty in getting fuel. The road became very bad and due to that, the tankers from Hohoe and Accra could not bring fuel to the town. Smugglers in fuel sold it at a very high price, so that the women couldn't afford to buy the fuel in order to operate the machine. So the profit they had made for the past six months was used for bread baking. Because they were only losing money on this project, they were not able to pay for the whole cost of the machine at the time expected.

Factor 13: Repair facilities and spare parts Who must repair the machines? What about her/his approachability? What about the supply of spare parts?

Weaving project Tanjigbe Dzabe is a town in the Ho District. A weaving project was started by the Women Association for Kente Weaving. The women showed much interest in this project. A loom was bought for them, a loan was acquired by the Non-Formal Education Division and they started production. Much profit was attained. But unfortunately the loom broke down. They tried to repair the loom, but the costs were too high.

   Therefore much money was spent and the women could not pay back the loan. The group also collapsed because some members distrusted the executive members.

Factor 14: Training on operation, maintenance and repair Are at least some of the women capable of maintaining and repairing the machine?

Palm digester A newly formed women's group decided to purchase a palm digester after an exposure tour to a Technology Fair. After a series of meetings, two leaders were sent for training on the use of the machine, maintenance and repair. Later on, other members were also given training. Each member was able to manipulate, maintain and repair the machine. There were also constant visits from a technician and there was service training for the group.

   This meant continuance in the operation of the machine, because all group members were involved and the group sustained.

Factor 15: Effects of the technology on the mechanized activity What are the changes caused by the tool with regard to the who, when and where of the activity?

Weanimix production This story is about a Weanimix production group at Yordan-nu in the Kpando District. Though the group has been in the Weanimix production for the last ten years, they never had their own corn mill. The group applied to a UNDP project for one. The mill was supplied to the group on credit. The women were trained in the operation and the maintenance of the machine. In addition they were also trained in record keeping, thus the management of the machine was in control of the women themselves. With the machine now in the village, they did not have to travel to other communities to have their Weanimix milled. This led to a decrease in production costs. The corn mill is serving the entire community, which has already accounted for an increase in income. As such, the women have been able to pay for the machine. The Weanimix project is still going on.

Factor 16: Effects of the technology on linked activities

Does the new technology have an impact on the activities done by the person herself, by family members or others? What about the impact on time and place of those activities?

Power tiller A women's group in Logba had an initial plan of establishing a group farm. Land was not readily available. So the group went to work on a farmer's plot for some fee. After some time, the farmer acquired a small power tiller with accessories, which he used in order to do a lot of work on his farm.

This technology, however useful it was to the farmer, cut the group off from their regular income.

Factor 19: The issue of control

Who will do the work, who will receive the income and who controls the income?

Grinding mill

1. *Who will do the work?* A grinding mill was donated by Unicef to the Savelegu Women's Group for income generation, for the improvement of their family living standards. The women nominated one member who operated the machine.
2. *Who will receive the income?* One group member collects the income and pays it to a treasurer.
3. *Who controls the income?* The women come together to decide on what to do with the income. They buy the fuel, spare parts and carry out maintenance of the machine.

In this project, the women are in total control and not the men. However, the men come in to help whenever it is necessary.

Factor 20: Social-cultural constraints

Are there any cultural or religious traditions which form constraints to the changes that come with the new technology?

Biogas for palm oil processing The women in the village of Apolonia were faced with a fuel wood problem for the processing of their palm oil in the Palm Oil Processing Project. A man, son of one of the women, had an idea for a biogas-plant. He called the women together and told them about the use of biogas. The women agreed to build a biogas plant. Because there were plenty of cows in the area, they thought this would be easy.

The plant was built with the help of the technical man. They had their fire working. Now they had to fetch cow dung to feed the plant. But everywhere they went, the cow-owners would not allow them to enter the kraal to collect the dung. This is due to the believe that a pregnant cow, who sees a woman, will have a miscarriage. Because no cow-owner would allow a woman to enter his kraal, the collecting of dung became a problem. The women could not use the biogas plant. Only women that can afford to pay young boys to do the collecting, are using the plant.

Bibliography

Ahmed, Iftikhar (ed.) (1985) *Technology and Rural Women: Conceptual and Empirical Issues*, Allen and Unwin, London.

Ahmed, Rehan (1998) *Ship and Port Waste Management in Pakistan*, WASTE (UWEP Case Study Series), Gouda.

Alkema, J. P., E. Baumann and W. Parmentier (1993) *Inkomensgenererende projecten, derde discussiestuk, kleinschalige bedrijvigheid*, TOOL, Amsterdam.

Almeyda, G. (1996) *Money Matters: Reaching Women Micro-entrepreneurs with Financial Services*, UN Development Fund for Women/Inter-American Development Bank, New York/Washington, DC.

Anderson, C. (1985) 'Small Scale Enterprise and Women', in C. Overholt, M. Anderson, K. Cloud and J. Austin (eds), *Gender Roles In Development Projects: A Casebook*, Kumarian Press, West Hartford, CT.

Appleton, H. (1993) 'Gender, Technology and Innovation', in *Appropriate Technology*, 20 (2).

— (1995) *Do It Herself: Women and Technical Innovation*, IT Publications, London.

Appropriate Technology International (1995) *Oilseed Press* No. 5, January, AT International, Washington, DC.

Arcens, Marie-Thérèse (1998) *Community Participation in Urban Solid Waste Management in Ouagadougou – Burkina Faso* (in French) ENDA/WASTE (UWEP Case Study Series), Gouda.

Arroyo, J., F. Rivas and I. Lardinois (eds) (1997/1998) *Solid Waste Management in Latin America – the Case of Small and Micro-enterprises and Co-operatives*, Urban Waste Series 5, co-publication with ACEPESA/IPES, Peru. (Spanish version, 1997; English version forthcoming.)

Asian Workshop (1990) *Asian Workshop: Technological Change and Women Towards the 21st Century*, Department of Science, Government of India, New Delhi.

Baffour-Awuah, Dan and Frances Minnow-Hagan (1994) *Study on the Provisions Of Improved Food Processing Equipment To Women's Groups in Ghana*, TOOL/FIT, Amsterdam.

Bantje, Han (1980) *Seasonal Variation in Birthweight Distribution in Ikwiriri Village*, BRALUP Research Paper No. 43, Dar es Salaam.

Bargel, G. (1990) *Was treibt die Muhlen an? Ein Fallbeispiel aus Afrika* (What keeps the mills going? An example from Africa), Family Planning Association of India, Panchkula, Haryana, India.

Baud, Isa (1989) *Forms of Production and Women's Labour: Gender Aspects of Industrialization in India and Mexico*, PhD dissertation, Technische Universiteit, Eindhoven.

Baud, Isa and G. A. de Bruijne (eds) (1993) *Gender, Small-scale Industry and Development Policy*, IT Publications, London.

Bhatt, E. (1989) *Grind of Work*, Self-Employed Women's Association (SEWA), Ahmedabad, India.

Bryceson, D. F. (1985) *Women and Technology in Developing Countries: Technological Change and Women's Capabilities and Bargaining Position*, UNCTAD/INSTRAW, Santo Domingo.

Bryceson, D. F. and J. Howe (1993) *Rural Household Transport in Africa: Reducing the Burden on Women?* ASC, Leiden.

Carr, M. (1984) *Blacksmith, Baker, Roofing-sheet Maker, Employment for Rural Women in Developing Countries*, IT Publications, London.

— (1985) *The AT Reader: Theory and Practice in Appropriate Technology*, ITDG Press, London.

— (1993) 'Women In Small-scale Industries, Some Lessons from Africa', in Baud and de Bruijne (eds).

Caubergs, Lisette (1991) *Women's Groups Managing Grainmills*, ATOL, Leuven.

CCIC (1991) *Two Halves Make a Whole: Balancing Gender Relations in Development*, Canadian Council for International Cooperation, Ottawa.

Centre of Science for Villages (1986) *Science and Technology for Women: Compendium of Technologies*, Department of Science and Technology, New Delhi.

Charlton, Sue Ellen M. (1984) *Women in Third World Development*, Westview Press, Boulder, CO.

Chen, Marty et al. (1986) *Indian Women. A Study of Their Role in the Dairy Movement*, Shakt Books, New Delhi.

Cowan, R. Schwartz (1983) *More Work for Mother: The Ironies of Household Technology from the Open Hearth to the Microwave*, Basic Books, New York.

Curtis, V. (1986) *Women and the Transport of Water*, Intermediate Technology Publications, London.

Damiba, Honorine (ongoing) *Household Garbage Collection around Ouagadougou*, Case Study for IFRTD Gender Issues in Rural Transport Programme.

Dankelman, Irene and Joan Davidson (1988) *Women and Environment in the Third World*, Earthscan, London.

Darrow, K., K. Keller and R. Pam (1981) *Appropriate Technology: A Source Book, Vol. II*, Volunteers in Asia Inc., Stanford, CA.

Dawson, J. and I. Barwell (1993) *Roads are Not Enough: New Perspectives on Rural Transport Planning in Developing Countries*, Intermediate Technology Publications, London.

Department of Science and Technology (1991–92) *Science and Technology for Women 1: Some Experiences in the Fisheries Sector*, Science and Society Division, Department of Science and Technology, Government of India, New Delhi.

Dholakia, Anila R. (1993) *Rural Women in Search of Sustainable Development: a Case Study in Grassroots Women's Natural Resources Management*, paper presented at the Indigenous Peoples' Symposium at Zuni, New Mexico, USA, July 1993.

D'Onofio-Flores, Pamela M. and Shela M. Pfafflin (eds) (1982) *Scientific-technological Change and the Role of Women in Development*, Westview Press, Boulder, CO.

Doran, J. (1996) *An Imbalanced Load: Gender Issues in Rural Transport Work*, draft paper prepared for ITDG, UK.

Downing, Jeannne (1991) 'Gender and the Growth of Microenterprises', *Small Enterprise Development*, 2 (1), March: 4–12.

ECART (1994) *Women and Food Processing in Sub-Saharan Africa, Proceedings of a Workshop Held in Accra, Ghana, 6–9 December 1994*, CTA, prepared for ECART by the Natural Resources Institute (NRI), Kent, UK.

Eigen, Johanna, (1992) 'Assistance to Women's Businesses – Evaluating the Options', *Small Enterprise Development* 3 (4): 4–14.

Everts, Saskia (1982), Marktvrouwen in Bobo-Dioulasso (Market Women in Bobo-Dioulasso), master's thesis, University of Groningen, Netherlands.

— (1995) *Tapping the Industry Channel, Opportunities for FIT for Assisting Women Food Processors in Kenya*, TOOLConsult, Amsterdam.

— (1997) *TOOL/TOOLConsult Conference 'Technology and Development: Strategies for the Integration of Gender' Amsterdam June 1997, Report*, TOOLConsult, Amsterdam.

Ewusi, Kodwo (1990) *Traditional and Improved Technologies for Food Processing for Rural Women in West Africa*, Tema Press, Tema, Ghana.

FAO (1990) *Gender Issues in Agriculture; Papers and Proceedings of the Regional Conference on Gender Issues in Agriculture, Manila, Philippines, 5–6 December 1990*, FAO, Rome.

— (1991) *The Impact of Technology on the Production Activities of Women in Latin America and the Caribbean*, Women in Agricultural Production and Rural Development Service, Institutions and Agrarian Reform Division, FAO, Rome.

— (1997) *Gender, Key to Sustainability and Food Security – From Words to Action, Plan of Action for Women in Development 1996–2001; Women and Population Division*, FAO, Rome.

Feldstein, Hilary Sims and Janice Jiggins (eds) (1994) *Tools for the Field: Methodologies Handbook for Gender Analysis in Agriculture*, Library of Management for Development series, Kumarian Press, West Hartford, CT.

Fellows, Peter and Ann Hampton (1992) *Small-scale Food Processing*, IT Publications, London.

Fernando, P. (1997) *Donkeys and Development: Socio-economic Issues in the Use and Management of Donkeys*, paper prepared for the ATNESA Workshop on Improving Donkey Utilization and Management, 5–9 May 1997, Zebre Zeit, Ethiopia.

Fernando, P. and Keter, S. (1996) *Internal Evaluation of IT Kenya's Rural Transport Programme*, Intermediate Technology Kenya, Nairobi (PO Box 39493, Nairobi, Kenya) and Intermediate Technology, Rugby (Myson House, Railway Terrace, Rugby CV21 3HT, UK).

Gemini (1994) *Micro- and Small-scale Enterprises in Kenya: Results of the 1993 Baseline Survey*, Bethesda, MD.

Gender Working Group, United Nations Commission on Science and Technology for Development (1995), *Missing Links, Gender Equity in Science and Technology for Development*, IDRC/ITPublications/UNIFEM, Ottawa/London/NewYork.

Gianotten, Vera, Verona Groverman, Edith van Walsum and Lida Zuidberg (1994)

Assessing the Gender Impact of Development Projects – Case Studies from Bolivia, Burkina Faso and India, KIT Publications, Amsterdam and IT Publications, London.

Giri, K. (1990) in H. Wallace, 'Appropriate Technology In Maternal and Child Health and Family Planning', in H. Wallace, *Health Care of Women and Children in Developing Countries*, Third Party Publishing Company, Oakland, CA, pp. 115–26.

Grijns, Mies et al. (1992) *Gender, Marginalisation and Rural Industries*, West Java Rural Non-farm Sector Research Project, Report Series No. RB-7.

Guijt, Irene (1994) *Questions of Difference: PRA, Gender and the Environment*, Training Manual, IIED, London.

Gupta, K. N. (1998) 'Excreta Collection in Ghaziabad, India', in Maria S. Muller (ed.), *The Collection of Household Excreta in Urban Low-income Settlements*, WASTE/ENSIC, Gouda and Bangkok.

Hilhorst, H. and H. Oppenoorth, (1992) *Financing Women's Enterprise, Beyond Barriers and Bias*, Royal Tropical Institute/IT Publications/UNIFEM, Amsterdam.

Holzner, Brigitte M. (1996) *Making Gender Policies Work in Development Organizations. Report of the Expert-meeting 'Successes and Limitations of Promoting a Gender Approach'*, Bilance and Vrouwenberaad Ontwikkelingssamenwerking, Oegstgeest.

Hombergh, Heleen van der (1993) *Gender, Environment and Development: a Guide to the Literature*, Institute for Development Research, Amsterdam.

Hook, W. (1994) *Counting on Cars, Counting out People: a Critique of the World Bank's Economic Assessment Procedures for the Transport Sector and Their Environmental Implications*, Paper No. I-0194, Institute for Transportation and Development Policy (ITDP), New York.

Huysman, Marijk (1994) 'Waste Picking as a Survival Strategy for Women in Indian Cities', *Environment and Urbanization*, 6 (2).

IIT India (1982) *Selected Technologies for Rural Women*, Centre for Rural Development and AT/Indian Institute of Technology, Ahmedabad.

Ilkkaracan, Ipek and Helen Appleton (1995) *Women's Roles in Technical Innovation*, IT Publications, London.

ILO (1983–86) Technology Series (including *Small Scale Processing of Fish* (No. 3), *Small Scale Weaving* (No. 4), *Small Scale Oil Extraction from Ground Nuts and Copra* (No. 5), *Small Scale Maize Milling* (No. 7), *Solar Drying: Practical Methods of Food Preservation*, ILO, Geneva.

— (1984) *Technological Change, Basic Needs and the Condition of Rural Women*, Report of the Joint ILO/Norway African Regional Project, ILO, Geneva.

— (1985) *Women Workers in Multinational Enterprises in Developing Countries*, Geneva, ILO.

— (1987) *Control and Management of Technology by Rural Women of Ghana*, ILO, Geneva.

ILO (1990) (originally 1984) *Improved Village Technology for Women's Activities, a Manual for West Africa*, ILO, Geneva.

ILO Jakarta (1993) *Gender Awareness and Planning Manual for Training of Trainers, Project Planners and Implementors in the Cooperative Sector*, ILO Cooperative Project Indonesia, Jakarta.

ILO and NCWD (1985–87) Technologies for Rural Women – Ghana: Technical

Manuals (including *Palm Oil Processing* (No. 1), *Gari Processing* (No. 4), *Coconut Oil Processing* (No. 5), ILO, Geneva.

Industrial Development Bank (1989) *Women in Food Processing Industry: A Survey in Gujarat*, Industrial Development Bank of India, Ahmedabad.

International Federation for Women in Agriculture (1997) *Environmentally Sound Technologies for Women in Agriculture*, International Federation for Women in Agriculture, New Delhi, India and International Institute of Rural Reconstruction, Silang, Cavite, Philippines

IT Publications (1998) *Appropriate Technology* 24 (4), March, IT Publications, London.

IT Transport Ltd (1996) *Promoting Intermediate Means of Transport: Approach Paper*, World Bank Sub Saharan Africa Transport Policy Programme SSATP Working Paper No. 20, World Bank, Washington DC.

IWTC (1986) *The Tech and Tools Book: a Guide to Technologies Women are Using World Wide*, IWTC, London.

Iyer, Lalitha (1991) *Women Entrepreneurs, Challenges and Strategies*, Friedrich Ebert Stiftung, New Delhi.

Jahan, Rounaq (1995) *The Elusive Agenda: Mainstreaming Women in Development*, Zed Books, London.

Jain, Devaki (1980) *Women's Quest for Power, Five Indian Case Studies*, Vikas Publishing House, Sahibadad.

Jain, S. C. (ed.) (1985) *Women and Technology*, Rawat Publications, Jaipur.

Jennings, M. (1992) *Study on the Constraints to Women's Use of Transport in Makate District, Tanzania*, ILO, Geneva.

Joss, S. (1989) *To Save Time: How the Nepalese Women's Development Programme has Reduced Rural Women's Labour Input in Everyday Tasks*, UNFPA, New York.

Keddie, J., S. Nanjundan and R. Tezler (1988) *Development of Rural Small Industrial Enterprise RSIE Study*, UNIDO, Vienna.

Kelkar, Govind (ed.) *Gender, Technology and Development Quarterly*, Sage, New Delhi.

Kettel, Bonnnie (1994) *Gender, Science and Technology in Development*, paper prepared for the seminar Wanita, Teknologi dan Pembangunan, Bandung, 20–22 April.

Kogi, Kazutaka, Wai-On Phoor and Joseph Thurmann (1989) *Low-cost Ways of Improving Working Conditions: 100 Examples from Asia*, ILO, Geneva.

Kristjanson, P., C. Wangia and J. Kashangaki (1995) *Agribusiness Subsector Study, Final Report*, USAID/Kenya Private Sector Office/Mwaniki Associates, Washington/Nairobi.

Lapid, Danilo G., Ligaya U. Munez and Lidel Lee I. Bongon (1998) *Community Participation in Urban Solid Waste Management in the Philippines*, UWEP Case Study Series, WASTE, Gouda.

Lingen, Annet (1994) *Gender Assessment Study: A Guide for Policy Staff*, DGIS, The Hague.

Lloyd-Laney, Megan (ed.) (1998) *Making Each and Every Farmer Count: Participation in Agricultural Engineering Projects*, FARMESA, Harare.

Luery, A. D., M. Bowman and Ch. A. Akinola (1992) *Technology and Women: Contradictions in the Process of Economic and Social Change. The Example of Cassava Processing, West Africa*, TechnoServe Inc., Norwalk, OH.

Ly, El Housseynou (1998) *Community Participation in Urban Solid Waste Management in Dakar – Senegal* (in French), ENDA/WASTE (UWEP Case Study Series), Gouda.

Macdonald, Mandy (ed.) (1994) *Gender Planning in Development Agencies. Meeting the Challenge*, Eurostep, Oxfam, Oxford.

Macdonald, Mandy, Ellen Sprenger and Ireen Dubel (1997) *Gender and Organizational Change: Bridging the Gap between Policy and Practice*, Royal Tropical Institute, Amsterdam.

Maldonado, C. and S. V. Sethurantan (1992) *Technological Capability in the Informal Sector. Metal Manufacturing in Developing Countries*, ILO, Geneva.

Malmberg, Calvo C. (1994a) *Case Atudy on Intermediate Means of Transport: Bicycles and Rural Women in Uganda*, SSATP Working Paper No. 12, World Bank, Washington, DC.

— (1994b) *Case Study on the Role of Women in Rural Transport: Access of Women to Domestic Facilities*, SSATP Working Paper No. 11, World Bank, Washington, DC.

March, Kathryn S. and Rachille L. Taggu (1986) *Women's Informal Associations in Developing Countries. Catalysts for Change?*, Westview Press, Boulder, CO.

Martinson, V. A. (1992) *Constraints to Adoption of New Technologies by Women in Developing Countries*, Working Paper No. 12, FAO Research Development Centre, Rome.

Mies, Maria and Vananda Shiva (1993) *Ecofeminism*, Zed Books, London.

Moser, Caroline, O. N. (1993) *Gender Planning and Development; Theory, Practice and Training*, Routledge, London.

Muech, Liesl (1995) 'Analyses of Entrepreneurship and Entrepreneurship Development', *Brainstorm* GTZ.CEFE, 1, 1995: 4–8.

Nanavaty, Reema and Purvi Buch (1990) *Salt Farmers of Santhalpur Taluka, Fieldstudy of Their Working and Living Conditions*, updated version (internal report) SEWA, Ahmedabad.

Ng Choon Sim, Cecilia (ed.) (1987) *Technology and Gender. Women's Work in Asia*, Univ. Paertanian, Selangor, Malaysia.

Oey-Gardiner, Mayling (1992) *Toward a Training Strategy to Improve The Welfare of Micro-enterprise Participants, With an Emphasis on the Position of Women*, World Bank Assistance Project to the Government of Indonesia, Jakarta.

Oost, E. C. J. van (1994) *Nieuwe functies, nieuwe verschillen. Genderprocessen in de constructie van de nieuwe automatiseringsfuncties 1955–1970*, Eburon, Delft.

Otero, Maria (1987) *Guidebook for Integrating Women Into Small and Micro Enterprise Projects*, USAID, Washington, DC.

Overholt, Catherine, Mary B. Anderson, Kathleen Cloud and James E. Austin (eds), (1985) *Gender Roles in Development Projects*, Kumarian Press, West Hartford, CT.

Page, B. (1996) 'Taking the Strain – The Ergonomics of Water Carrying', *Waterlines* 14 (3), January.

Parikh, Indira J. (1991) *Women in Management in India*, Indian Institute of Management, Working Paper No. 979, Ahmedabad.

Parikh, Indira J. and Nayana A. Shah (1991) *Women Managers in Transition: From Homes to Corporate Offices*, Indian Institute of Management, Ahmedabad, Working Paper No. 941.

Parikh, P. P. and S. P. Sukhatme (1992) *Women Engineers in India*, IIT, Bombay.

Parker, Rani (1993) *Another Point of View: A Gender Analysis Training Manual for Grassroots Workers*, UNIFEM, New York.

Pruyne, E. (1993) *An End to Debt, Operational Guidelines for Credit Projects*, UNIFEM, New York.

Rao, N. (1993) 'Mobility for Rural Women: a Cycling Campaign in South India', article written as a case study for inclusion in UNIFEM *Rural Transport Sourcebook*.

— (ongoing) *Transport and Gender Relations: Santhal Women of South Bihar*, case study for IFRTD Gender Issues in Rural Transport programme.

Rao, A., M. Anderson and C. Overholt (1991) *Gender Analysis in Development Planning: a Case Book*, Kumarian Press, West Hartford, CT.

Royal Netherlands Embassy India (1993) *The Emerging Power, Women in the Indo-Dutch Water Supply and Sanitation Projects*, Directorate General for International Cooperation, Royal Netherlands Embassy, New Delhi, India.

Sainath, P. (1995) 'Where There is a Wheel', *Humanscape*, July.

Savara, M. and C. R. Sridhar (1994) *Impact of the Medleri Charkha*, SHAKTI, The Social Research Centre, Bombay.

Schoemaker, Annemieke and Katja Jassey (eds) (1996) *Proceedings from Agrotec/FAO Workshop Gender and Agricultural Engineering, held at Kadoma Ranch Motel, Zimbabwe 4–8 March 1996*, FAO, Rome.

Sen, Gita and Caren Grown (1987) *Development, Crises and Alternative Visions*, Monthly Review Press, New York.

SEWA (1988) *SEWA in 1988*, SEWA, Ahmedabad.

Shamsi, Sohail and Rehan Ahmed (1998) *Community Participation in Urban Solid Waste Management in Karachi – Pakistan*, WASTE (UWEP Case Study Series), Gouda.

Shiva, Vandana (1989) *Staying Alive: Women, Ecology and Development*, Zed Books, London.

Sieber, N. (1996) *Rural Transport and Rural Development: the Case of the Makate District, Tanzania*, Karlsruhe Papers in Economic Policy Research, Vol. 4, Nomos Verlag, Baden-Baden.

Sjaifudian, Hetifah (1992) 'Women as Family Workers', in Grijns et al. (eds), *Gender, Marginalisation and Rural Industries*, pp. 175–192.

Srivastava (1985) 'Harnessing Technology for Improving the Quality of Life of Rural Women', in Jain (1985)*Women and Technology*, pp. 38–74.

Stamp, Patricia (1989) *Technology, Gender and Power in Africa*, IDRC, Ottawa.

Tanburn, Jim (1995) *Report on FIT Implementation Mission #6 to Kenya, 26 March to 8 April 1995*, FIT/ILO, Geneva.

Tanburn, Jim and Peter van Bussel (1995) *The Potential for Development of Improved Agricultural Equipment by Jua Kali Metal Workers: a Case Study in Embu, Kenya*, FIT/ILO, Geneva.

Tempelman, Diana (1996), *Observations Concerning the Workshop 'Introducing Technology to Women's Enterprisese', Organised by TechnoServe-Ghana/TOOLConsult-Netherlands, 30 September–4 October 1996, Sunyani, Brong Ahafo Region, Ghana*, FAO, Accra.

Thomas-Slayter, Barbara, Rachel Polestico, Andrea Lee Esser, Octavia Taylor and Elvina Mutua (1995) *A Manual for Socio-Economic and Gender Analysis: Responding to the Development Challenge*, ECOGEN research project, Clark University, Worcester, MA.

Tinker, Irene (1987) 'The Human Economy of Microentrepreneurs', paper presented at the International Seminar on Women in Micro- and Small-Scale Enterprise Development, Ottawa, Canada, 26 October 1987.

TOOL (1994) *Development, Introduction and Dissemination of the Medleri Charkha, a Self-winding Foot-operated Spinning Wheel*, TOOL, Amsterdam.

Townsend, Janet (1988) *Women in Developing Countries: A Selected Annotated Bibliography*, Institute of Development Studies, Sussex.

UNDP (1995) *Human Development Report*, UN, New York.

UNICEF (1983) *Simple Technologies for Rural Women in Bangladesh*, UNICEF, Bangladesh Women's Development Programme.

UNIFEM (1987–93) Food Cycle Technology Source Books, UNIFEM, New York.

— (1990a) *Strategies for the Dissemination of Appropriate Technologies to Rural Women: An Overview*, UNIFEM, New York.

— (1990b) *Filling the Information Gap: How Do Women Get Information on the Technologies Appropriate to Their Needs* (Internal publication), UNIFEM, New York.

— (1990c) *UNIFEM's Experience With Women and Food Technology Programmes in Africa*, internal publication, UNIFEM, New York.

— (1994) *Review of UN Agency Activities in the Field of Gender, Science and Technology*, UNIFEM, New York.

— (1996–98) Energy and Environment Technology Resource Books: *Rural Transport*; *Water Supply*; *Energy Saving in Small Scale Enterprises*; *Electricity for Households*, UNIFEM, New York.

Veken, Mieke van der and Itziar Hernandez (1986) *Women, Technology and Development*, ATOL, Leuven.

Vickers, Jeanne (1991) *Women and the World Economy*, Women and World Development Series, Zed Books, London.

Voeten, Jaap (ed.) (1993) *Report of Symposium 'Beyond Sub-Contracting, Assessing Linkages Between Large and Small Enterprises as Small-Scale Enterprise Development Mechanisms'*, Royal Tropical Institute (KIT), Amsterdam.

Voorlichtingsdienst Ontwikkelingssamenwerking ministerie van Buitenlandse Zaken (1991) Kleinschalige bedrijvigheid, DGIS, Den Haag.

White, Benjamin (1992) 'Studying Women and NonFarm Rural Sector Development', in B. Kettel, F. Carden and J. Soemirat (eds), *The ITB–York University Forum on Gender and Development, December 1990*, Research Paper #35, Pusat Penelitian Lingkungan Hidup, Institut Teknologi Bandung, Bandung.

Williams, Suzanne with Janet Seed and Adelina Mwau (1994) *The Oxfam Gender Training Manual*, Oxfam, Oxford.

Zimmerman, J. (1983) *The Technological Woman: Interfacing with Tomorrow*, Praeger, New York.

Zoomers, E. B. (1993) 'Appropriate Technology: Is It Right for Small Business?' *Small Enterprise Development*, IT Publications, London.

Index

Books of related interest from Zed

Abortion in the Developing World
  Edited by Axel I. Mundigo and Cynthia Indriso

African Women and Development: A history
  Margaret C. Snyder and Mary Tadesse

*Between Monsters, Goddesses and Cyborgs: Feminist confrontations with science, medicine
  and cyberspace*
  Edited by Nina Lykke and Rosi Braidotti

Biopolitics: A feminist and ecological reader
  Edited by Vandana Shiva and Ingunn Moser

Empowerment and Women's Health: Theory, methods, and practice
  Jane Stein

Feminist Perspectives on Sustainable Development
  Edited by Wendy Harcourt

*Gender and Development in the Arab World: Women's economic participation: patterns
  and policies*
  Edited by Nabil F. Khoury and Valentine M Moghadam

Gender, Education and Development
  Edited by Christine Heward and Sheila Bunwaree

Getting Institutions Right for Women in Development
  Edited by Anne-Marie Goetz

Monitoring Family Planning and Reproductive Rights: A manual for empowerment
  Anita Hardon, Ann Mutua, Sandra Kabir and Elly Engelkes

Negotiating Reproductive Rights: Women's perspectives across countries and cultures
  Edited by Rosalind P. Petchesky and Karen Judd/IRRRAG

Promoting Gender Equality at Work: Turning vision into reality for the 21st century
  Edited by Eugenia Date-Bah

The Elusive Agenda: Mainstreaming women in development
  Rounaq Jahan

The Power to Change: Women in the third world redefine their environment
  Women's Feature Service

The Strategic Silence: Gender and Economic Policy
  Edited by Isabella Bakker

The Women, Gender and Development Reader
    Edited by Nalini Visvanathan with Lynn Duggan, Laurie Nisonoff
    and Nan Wiegersma

Women and Empowerment: Participation and decision-making
    Prepared by Marilee Karl

Women and Work
    Prepared by Susan Bullock

These books should be available from all good bookshops. In case of difficulty, please contact us: Zed Books Ltd, 7 Cynthia St, London NI 9JF, UK.

tel: +44 (0)171 837 4014; Fax +44 (0)171 833 3960
e-mail: sales@zedbooks.demon.co.uk